# FRANKEN SCOOTERS
## to
# Dracula's castle

FINGERS IN PIES
PUBLICATIONS

British Library Cataloguing in Publication Data
**Published by:** Fingers In Pies Publications
**Address:** PO Box 46, Weston-super-Mare, BS231AF
**Contact:** 01934 417834
**www.scooterproducts.com**

**ISBN:** 978-0-9548216-2-3

**Printed by:** Pensord Press 01495 223721

# ACKNOWLEDGEMENTS:

**Beta reading and editorial suggestions:**
Dean Orton, Chris Caldwell, Nigel Ellis, Julie Round, Thomas H Green

**Proof reading:**
Wendy Hughes, Julie Round & Nicola Roe

**Additional photography:**
Kimberly Orton, Sam Round, Lee O'Neill, Ian Blackett and Dean Orton

**Front cover design:**
Lee Daniels (leandiesel.com)

**Mapping:** StepMap.com

**Technical and product support for this trip:**
Readspeed Scooters, Rimini Lambretta Centre,
Putoline Lubricants, Xena Locks, Interphone Intercoms
Shoei Helmets, Weise jackets & gloves, Drayko Kevlar jeans,
Draggin' jeans, Tucano Urbano jackets and gloves, Salomon boots,
Custom Chrome Exhausts (Nuneaton).

# CONTENTS

# PROLOGUE

There are easier ways of crossing continents than using half-century old scooters. Equally, mountaineering would be so much easier if you could just get a helicopter to drop you at the summit. That's not really the point though, is it?

Achieving targets by taking the easy option is boring. Where's the novelty in walking from Land's End to John o'Groats when hundreds have done it before you? However, if you run the length of Britain carrying a fridge, like charity fundraiser 'Tony the Fridge' did in 2013, then suddenly it becomes newsworthy.

The unique element of our ride to Istanbul – which scooter riders have tackled in the past – would be our choice of steed. Neither my Lambretta nor my wife's Maicoletta have been left standard. Instead they are Frankenstein's monsters: unique hybrids of scooter chassis and motorcycle engine cobbled together with many one-off parts and garden shed ingenuity.

There's a certain level of responsibility involved when your entire family sets off on a ride to the next continent on a collection of bits you've built or assembled with your own hands. In the months of preparation in the shed, I wondered if our mutated classic scooters would prove to be as good as the factory originals.

Therein lay our challenge, and also the metaphorical fridge on my back.

# PRELUDE

I saw the Harley Davidson in the distance pulling up to the traffic lights before the motorway slip road.

'Let's have some fun.'

Fun, in this instance, came in the form of a scooter I'd just built for my wife, Tracy, to ride on a forthcoming odyssey to Istanbul; a big, hulking rarity called a Maicoletta, produced in 1959. Its German manufacturers, Maico, would go on to become leading players in the Motocross world until the Japanese overtook them, in every sense.

This was no standard Maicoletta though. It was bought without its original 277cc two-stroke engine and instead I'd surgically inserted a 40hp 400cc 4-stroke Japanese enduro engine. That's lots of numbers, 4s mostly, but not many compared to a Harley. Still, it should be enough to give the rider a shock if he was slow off the lights.

Never underestimate the acceleration of a Harley; they may not be aerodynamic but 1,340cc is a big engine for a motorcycle and the throbbing V-twin produces ample torque. In the first few feet the Harley rider knew something was wrong, so he wound on a fistful of throttle. I didn't manage to lead him from the green light, but I kept up all the way up the slip-road. At 75mph he thought he'd done enough and glanced in his mirrors, but the old scooter was still there, accelerating. His response was to blast out into the fast lane at speed to overtake a few cars. Then he pulled back into the left lane at a steady 70mph; which is as fast as you want to cruise on a Harley without any form of wind protection. No doubt he thought that was a sufficient buffer to stamp his authority.

My plan was to sail past him at top speed, sat bolt upright. I knew that the Maicoletta would easily do 85mph before its primitive suspension started squirming like an eel posted through a letterbox.

As I drew alongside though, things didn't feel right. The Suzuki engine – which had been perfectly smooth on Tracy's first test ride to Santa Pod drag race track a week earlier – now felt extremely rough. It was making all kinds of knocking noises when I opened it up. Rather than making a triumphant and impressive overtake, I could only creep past on the unhappy Maico before veering off at the very next exit. There was no victorious elation when I pulled into a convenient lay-by, only the grim foreboding of mechanical disaster. The engine ticked over fine but it knocked horribly when I revved it. Glancing behind I could now see that the exhaust was belching clouds of white smoke whenever I commanded any revs.

I switched the motor off to prevent further damage and looked around to locate the problem. A tiny drip of coolant from the radiator hoses splashed onto the tarmac below the scooter. That wasn't right. I tugged it to check the security of the connection but the hose came off in my hand, spewing a hot cocktail of water and antifreeze all over the lay-by.

'Bollocks', I muttered, as the significance of my actions finally dawned. Our departure to Turkey is next month and I'd just blown up the freshly-rebuilt engine by racing motorbikes on the motorway. Six months of intense work unravelled like a jumper caught on a nail, all because I couldn't resist a race.

Bollocks, bollocks, bollocks.

Jerome, the jovial proprietor of Readspeed Scooters in Stourport-on-Severn, took the news on the chin when I phoned him. He'd built the engine once and to do it again would be 'no sweat'.

At home I'd stripped off the head and cylinder but couldn't see what was wrong apart from all the components being oily and black. Jerome assessed everything and rebuilt the engine with new valves.

'It'll be fine', he assured me.

With only a few weeks left before our departure I returned the engine to its snug new home in the Maicoletta frame and tried again. It wasn't fine. The engine ran as rough as an elephant's scrotum; misfiring and smoking.

Bollocks, in fact, big hairy elephant bollocks.

While testing the engine a small amount of fuel dribbled out of the carburettor onto the workbench, but it hadn't evaporated in the way petrol is supposed to do. I dipped my gloved index finger into the liquid, rubbed it against my thumb and held it under my nose. Something wasn't right.

Minutes later I had confirmation in the form of a receipt from my wallet. Two miles prior to my race with the Harley I'd topped up the fuel tank, but the receipt clearly stated that I'd added 3.2 litres of Fuelsave Diesel, not petrol. This was one of those moments where you feel like pummelling your own face with a cricket bat.

Thankfully I did not have a cricket bat to hand, only a hammer. Filling up from the wrong fuel pump didn't really call for that. Not quite.

Miraculously, with the tank and carburettor flushed out and given a fresh drink of neat petrol, the engine ran beautifully. As it should, after the second rebuild in only a month.

I begged forgiveness from Jerome, but as ever he was philosophical about the situation. At least the engine now had fresh valves, so he had more confidence that the Maico would survive the trip. We might be behind schedule, but at least we were back on track for Istanbul.

*One dead Maicoletta 400: time to phone a friend.*

# ORIGIN OF SPECIES

In the automotive ocean, two-stroke scooters are plankton. Simple single-cylinder organisms capable of enormous feats and distances, while trying not to be devoured by the blue whale of a petrol tanker or snapped up by a shark-like sports car.

It's not easy to explain a love affair with vintage Italian scooters to anyone who cannot appreciate the sleek lines of a Lambretta; penned by supercar stylists like Pininfarina or Bertone. These designers were the Michelangelos of the 20th century. They used their innate sense of art and proportion not to fulfil Vatican commissions for frescos on the Sistine Chapel, but to style vehicles for the major families of the Italian automotive industry. One month that might mean drawing a swish new car for Enzo Ferrari, but if the next job came from Ferdinando Innocenti then the same design flair would be applied to a scooter.

Lambretta scooters produced in the Swinging Sixties are automotive artworks by the best men in the business. Vespa scooters – arguably – are better transport. They are more comfortable, more reliable and infinitely simpler in both chassis and motor than a Lambretta. A 1960s Vespa has fewer moving parts in its entire engine than there are in just the drive chain of a comparable Lambretta. I love both brands, but I still prefer the slim styling of a Lambretta, despite their many mechanical flaws. These are creases that I've spent a lifetime trying to iron out.

I grew up – again arguably – in the 1980s Scooterboy scene of Margaret Thatcher's Britain. This truly underground cult may have roots in the late '70s revival of the Sixties Mod movement, but the style and fashions were very different.

The accepted definition of Mod – 'clean living in difficult circumstances' – is open-ended. It means someone who makes an effort to look sharp and care for their appearance, no matter how hard they work, or how hard they party. That definition of Mod does not say anything about having to look like an aging member of the Quadrophenia re-enactment society. Nor does it make any mention of transport.

The 1980s Scooterboy scene was all about the transport, with zero regard for clean living under any circumstances. For many teenagers like me, who felt restricted by the narrow definitions of Mod, mutating into a Scooterboy was a liberating experience. You could now wear what you wanted and listen to whatever music you liked. Your only tie to the 20,000 other party animals who descended on Isle of Wight National Scooter Run in 1984 was your choice of transport. The broad, ill-defined envelope of 'Scooterboy' contained punks, hippies, skinheads, football casuals and everything in between. In fact, even people who liked Spandau Ballet, for heaven's sake.

The only cohesive element was the ownership of a scooter, and a desire to ride it around the country making new friends and getting off your nut with them. It was this eclectic, anti-conformist mix that really appealed to my rebellious side. Admittedly there was a uniform in the form of the MA1 flight jacket with sewn-on Paddy Smith rally patches, but that was purely optional. This lack of clear definition is perhaps why such a massive British youth cult has had so little media recognition beyond Gareth Brown's tome 'Scooter Boys'.

One typical Scooterboy belief is that you can – once armed with a selection of blunt screwdrivers, rusty spanners and dangerous cutting tools – improve both the performance and styling of your scooter. It is testament to the simplicity of the two-stroke engine that the former is actually true, and even now you can 'bolt-on' a 30% power increase to a Vespa PX simply by fitting a £200 exhaust system and adjusting the carburettor to suit. Try that with a superbike!

As for improving on the styling of classic Italian scooters with only the use of an angle grinder and some half-spent rattle cans from your dad's shed; let's just say that many have tried and few succeeded, but each attempt is a personalisation.

Rather than worrying that any modification to our chosen transport would diminish its value or invalidate the insurance, Scooterboys went to town on personalisation. Whether the result has any artistic merit is down to the eye of the beholder, but at least a customised scooter is a reflection of the owner's personality rather than some bland, standard vehicle distinguishable from many others only by the characters on the number plate.

There is a common misconception amongst people weaned on capitalist culture that when you finally buy the car or house of your dreams, only then you have 'made it'. That is, until you yearn for your next dream object. Is that state of constant dissatisfaction any way to live?

Far more gratifying, and far truer to the original sense of 'made it', is to actually make it: if you have the skills then build what you want with your own hands, or at least assemble it. Even if you have something customised to your own tastes by an artisan: as long as you have more input to the creative process than picking your vehicle from the manufacturer's standard colour range, then you have customised your vehicle. Rather than simply *owning* it until it is discarded, like a pair of shoes, it *belongs* to you like a dog. The difference is subtle but immense.

*With Sam on my 250cc Lambretta in April 2006.*

11

# MY SCOOTER:
# A LAMBRETTA WITH HONDA POWER

I may be in my forties but Scooterboy blood (a hazardous concoction unsuitable for transfusion to infidels) still flows through my veins. I continue to believe that my breed – armed now with better tools and more experience – can improve on the standard scooter.

My day job as a writer and photographer for Scootering – the world's longest running scooter magazine – has introduced me to many similarly afflicted nutcases over the years. I was once tasked with interviewing the inventor of the 'world's first inflatable scooter'. This eventually turned out to be a collection of tubing and a strimmer engine fitted with a large orange whoopee cushion by a charming old nutcase from the Caribbean. Only a little further down my list of mental scooter builders is Frank Sanderson. He is the Isambard Kingdom Brunel of the scooter modification world, churning out radical engine-transplant projects from a windswept farm near Preston.

Frank was involved with Alan Rosser in the ill-fated 'Rossa 350' enterprise in the late 1980s which shoehorned Yamaha RD350 YPVS engines into Lambretta chassis. Only twelve of these ridiculously fast twin-cylinder scooters were completed before Rosser used the deposits he'd taken for many others to do a moonlight flit to New Zealand. Eventually, upon return to the UK, Mr Rosser returned to his dodgy dealings. He was eventually killed in 1999 by a gunshot to the head courtesy of persons unknown.

Thankfully, Frank saw the writing on the wall and bailed out of the Rossa business before everything went pear-shaped. Like Dr Frankenstein though, he continued to dream about building mescaline-fuelled mutant mopeds.

In the year 2000 Frank collaborated on a new project called the RX250. This was a Lambretta that retained all the original bodywork, but hidden within was an insane 43hp 250cc Rotax kart engine capable of well over 100mph.

I tested it, I loved it, I wanted it.

Actually I didn't want an RX250, because there's no time in my life for a toy so fragile or impractical. I needed something with the same layout, but with a more practical engine capable of higher mileages with less maintenance. In 2005 I finally set about getting just that.

Having hunted around for months for a suitable donor I eventually settled on the Honda CRM 250 enduro bikes produced from 1989 to 1999. These were never officially sold in the UK by Honda, but many used examples have been imported from Japan and sold to British enthusiasts who appreciate their Tonka-like build quality.

The CRM had all the features I was looking for: a compact two-stroke engine, six gears, a balance shaft to reduce vibration and most importantly an oil pump. The pump was top of my shopping list because it mixes 2-stroke engine lubricant with fuel as it enters the engine, rather than having to manually pour oil into the fuel tank at every petrol stop, as you must on standard Lambretta. That is a dreary, repetitive and fundamentally dirty job that I look forward to with the same enthusiasm as pulling tangled hairs from a blocked shower.

In 2005 I managed to buy a well-used CRM 250 from an oik in Northampton who casually mentioned that he hated scooters. After loading his pride and joy into my van I took great delight in explaining that I was going to cut his bike into pieces and turn it into a scooter. He wasn't happy.

Once all the other donor parts were gathered for the project I transported them to Frank's Lancashire lab, where the pile of metal was converted through a mixture of fabrication and black magic, into a rolling chassis. From there I took over building it into a complete scooter.

I've never been one for shiny paint because it's too easy to scratch and my scooters are built to be used. Instead the 'Series 6' started out in satin black and the only thing I've added since are stickers and a thick film of dead insects. The scooter has been used for rallies in Britain, Sweden, Germany, France, Belgium, Italy, Holland and Spain. Apart from a few initial teething troubles it has proved miraculously reliable.

Maybe not miraculously, because the engine was built by Honda who are famed for employing the most dedicated and thorough engineers in the business, producing the motorcycle equivalents of Swiss watches.

As a company I'm not a big fan of Honda: they are corporate bullies who pushed for the extinction of the 2-stroke engine, despite the fact that their grip on the technology was pretty good. The CRM proves that.

What does Honda know about the needs of a Scooterboy though? It is in our genetic make-up to meddle, even with near-perfection. Pretty soon I'd developed my own 300cc conversion kit for the engine which produced even more power but was thirstier and more vibratory. I loved the additional torque of 'my' conversion, but for the purposes of this trip I conceded that Mr Honda does in fact know best, and put the engine back to standard 250cc format.

*If you want a crazy Lambretta 'talk to Frank':*
*my 250 taking shape in 2005.*

# TRACY'S SCOOTER: A MAICOLETTA WITH SUZUKI POWER

Having built a quick, reliable but standard looking scooter it was natural that my wife Tracy – who shares my scooter addiction – should want something similar. We both have fast, large capacity modern automatic scooters in the garage that would be better suited to such a trip, but they do not stir the soul like something old and built from scratch.

Typically Tracy had very specific demands. She wanted something at least as powerful as mine, but preferably more comfortable and with the convenience of electric start. Her petite frame is not best suited to a battle of wills with the kickstart of a reluctant single-cylinder engine.

Two-strokes that have both oil injection and electric start are extremely rare beasts. That is why we ended up looking towards bigger 4-stroke motors, and consequently then to bigger scooters. We needed something that could house such an engine without it poking out of the bodywork like a tumour.

The massive German Maicoletta seemed like an ideal candidate because it was originally built with a motorcycle style engine and chain drive. However, in order to use the original wheel and swinging arm I needed to find an engine with the drive chain on the right. That is the 'European' side, and a very rare configuration nowadays. BMW's F650 Funduro single appeared to be the perfect donor because its Austrian-made Rotax engine would just about fit under the bodywork. Or so it appeared.

We duly bought an engineless Maicoletta and a running BMW F650 to strip for parts. As before, I took the accumulated mess of metal up to Frank in Preston for the magic wand treatment.

Frank and side-kick Chris balanced the Rotax engine on blocks of wood, measured things with tape measures and pulled the kind of faces that plumbers pull before they hand you an extortionate bill.

The Rotax 650 engine, they concluded, was just too big.

"You need a smaller engine", said Frank, frankly, "something like a 400".

Annoyingly this meant reassembling the BMW and selling it on eBay. Instead we bought a complete Suzuki DRZ400E from another oik, this time from a sink-hole estate in Sheffield. This competition 'E' version of the enduro engine makes almost as much power as the Rotax 650, but importantly it is around 30% smaller.

With such a compact power-plant the conversion looked so much simpler that I decided to tackle it myself, with the help of local metal molester Range, machinist Phil March and our friend Ellis for the paintwork.

"This is going to be easy", I assured Tracy, confidently.

It wasn't easy.

I spent most of the next six months in the shed, surrounded by sparks, oil, fumes and a fog of industrial-grade profanities. Every escapable social function was sacrificed in order to build the Maicitbetta (Tracy's word-play on 'Make it Better' and 'Maicoletta') and still have enough time to iron out any bugs before our journey.

The build required fabrication of a completely new swinging arm and exhaust system, and extensive modification to the rear wheel and fuel tank. The most involved part was converting the forks and front drum wheel to accept the massive disc brake required to stop a heavy scooter capable of over 90mph.

I can't have done too bad a job because Tracy rode the Maicitbetta to its first event at Santa Pod in June without incident. Then the following week, while on my way to another shake-down scooter rally, I decided to race a Harley Davidson after filling the fuel tank with diesel...

But you already know that bit.

*Maicitbetta on the operating table. (Photo: Lee O'Neill)*

*Drag racing Maicitbetta at Santa Pod. (Photo: Ian Blackett)*

# FIVE GO MAD IN EASTERN EUROPE

At this point I need to introduce the other players in our merry band, for we never planned to travel alone. The third scooter in the pack belonged to our old friend, Dean Orton, proprietor of Rimini Lambretta Centre. It shouldn't be too taxing to guess what brand of scooter he would be taking.

Quite how a Mod from the arse end of Cornwall came to run a world class restoration business in the hills near Rimini is a tale in itself. The short version is that you don't achieve such things without hard work, intelligence and an adventurous spirit. Unlike many scooter shop owners who once raced or rallied, but have given it up in favour of grumbling from behind a counter, Dean still practices what he preaches. He's ridden scooters from Italy to England many times, and ventured as far east as the Ukraine by Lambretta.

Quite independently, Dean had planned to ride to Istanbul earlier in 2013 with some Italian friends. On finding this out, we instead decided to join forces and follow Dean's suggested route to Turkey via the former communist states of Slovenia, Hungary, Romania and Bulgaria. It had never been my intention to head so far out of our way, and the time required to do this meant compromises to our plan. With Tracy having only a month off work we would not have sufficient time to ride all the way from England, so instead we chose to transport our scooters to Italy and ride with Dean from there.

My only concern with this enlarged party was that our 11-year-old son Sam would be riding pillion on my Lambretta. I wondered if it was unfair to upset the equilibrium of a 'lad's outing' by introducing a child into the mix.

On the whole Italians are far more comfortable bringing kids into adult environments than stuffy Britons, but even so, I didn't want to cramp anyone's style. Dean however took this as an opportunity to reset the balance by bringing his 12-year-old daughter Kimberly on the back of his scooter. Then, as is often the way with grand plans, Dean's friends dropped out one by one due to family commitments, until we were a group of five on three scooters.

The mathematically astute amongst you will realise that this number is not ideal for foreign travel. If there were six of us on four scooters for example, then there would be the option to leave a broken scooter and still transport everyone to the next destination. Our current configuration left us without that possibility; therefore a breakdown was something we really could not afford. Maybe radically-modified scooters were not the most sensible things to take then?

Ah, bollocks, we'd be fine.

*Sam and Kimberly: contributing photographers for this book.*

# WON'T SOMEBODY PLEASE THINK OF THE CHILDREN!

At this point it's only fair to mention that no children were in any way coerced into taking part in this silly adventure. Both kids have grown up around scooters all their lives. Sam was riding pillion on my Lambretta chopper at the age of three, and shortly after her birth Kimberly first rode with her mother Isabella in Dean's Lambretta sidecar outfit.

For both kids, getting on the back of a scooter is a normal form of transport, and one that they are both keen to ride as soon as they are old enough to get a licence. What seems unfair is that Kimberly only has to wait a year until her 14th birthday before she can ride a 50cc scooter in Italy, while UK legislation requires that Sam will have to wait until he is 16.

Don't get the impression that our progeny are the sort of mini-me skinheads occasionally found on the rallies, complete with shaved heads, wearing Crombie coats or flight jackets covered in scooter patches. I've never encouraged Sam to come on the rallies with us: quite the opposite. The scooter rallies are where I go to behave like a child, not to have the responsibility of looking after one. However those infrequent weekends spent at his grandparents while we ride off to a rally have made him inquisitive. He's desperate to get a scooter and be part of the gang, and I respect that.

Admittedly there are risks in taking kids on the back of scooters, but there are risks in anything you do. Alternatively, you could try to wrap your children in cotton wool and keep them in a cupboard for their own safety, but Social Services will eventually find out and set them free. Still, it's something to bear in mind as a cost-effective alternative to a baby-sitter.

I don't class myself as a good teacher, but at the very least I want to give my son some experience and an understanding that life is not confined to a home town or the local belief system. There is a world beyond our borders, and beyond the nearest screen, where geography, history, politics and religion knit together in different configurations to give each place its own identity.

Occasionally I pondered if I was being reckless by taking my son to such remote places, but a story from the town of my birth reassures me that there is more danger in a restricted world view.

I was born in Hartlepool on England's North East coast: a town which is famous for one event and little else. During the Napoleonic wars a French ship reputedly ran aground off the fishing town in a severe storm. The devastation was total, with the only survivor washed ashore amongst the wreckage being a monkey, dressed for the amusement of the crew in a French sailor's uniform.

The story goes that the people of Hartlepool, who were not well-travelled folk, and likely influenced by damning anti-French propaganda cartoons, took the monkey to be a Frenchman. The monkey was then charged with the crime of spying by a kangaroo court convened on the beach. Unable to defend himself against these allegations – on account of being a monkey – the good people of Hartlepool found the poor simian guilty and hung him from an improvised gallows constructed on the beach.

Whether the story is true can never be proved, but the people of Hartlepool don't deny it. In fact they take a strange civic pride in this tale of provincial ignorance. From my perspective the story acts as a powerful reminder that travel is an education in itself, and that you should always question propaganda. There's no substitute for seeing something with your own eyes, and no better way to see it than on two wheels.

# PREPARATION H

There are various ways of preparing for a trip like this. You can do a lot of planning or you can put your trust in good fortune and simply follow where your nose takes you. A compromise between the two is probably best.

Our initial plan was adjusted more than a prison Rubik's Cube. Dean's original idea was ambitious enough to visit Ukraine, before we realised that the additional mileage would make this less a relaxing tour and more of a race from one point to another.

One of our scooter club-mates – Dave Fowler – sadly died in 1996 following an accident on his Vespa. His scooter carried stickers which read: 'Along the way take time to smell the flowers'. That is good advice, particularly for those who've lived in a big city and still suffer from terminal impatience.

Taking time to smell the flowers appears to be a growing movement, particularly amongst older sportsbike riders who've spent their lifetime racing from place to place, only to realise that they've seen nothing but smeared streaks of landscape in their peripheral vision. Validating this theory, a friend recently bumped into a group of British riders in France who'd forsaken their usual superbikes in favour of touring on 90cc Honda step-thrus. They'd made this seemingly retrograde step in order to take in the countryside that they were riding through. That's not as daft as it seems.

Dean was clearly working from the same perspective when he chose his steed for the journey; a Lambretta Grand Prix 150 made under licence by Scooters India Limited (SIL) in the 1990s.

When Italian Lambretta manufacturers Innocenti quit the scooter market in 1971 the entire production line and all the spare parts were sold to India, where the last Lambretta model – the Grand Prix (or DL in Italy) – soldiered on until the end of the '90s despite infrequent upgrades and dubious build quality.

This particular scooter came to him with only 115km on the speedo. It had previously been the property of Italian accessory manufacturer – Vigano – who bought it to star in a promotional 'glamour' calendar which they never completed.

Despite it being basically a new scooter, Dean is not one to leave things to chance. All the running gear was upgraded, new cables were fitted and the rims were swapped for modern tubeless alloy wheels from German firm SIP, in the interests of safety.

Dean didn't exactly go overboard on engine tuning though, increasing the capacity only as far as 186cc with the fitment of a 'Mugello' tuning kit coupled with a 'Gori' sports exhaust. With only around 9hp on tap this would be no road rocket, however its saving grace would be the fitment of Dean's own innovation: the Cyclone 5-speed gearbox. This upgrade from the original 4-speed – developed in conjunction with Denis Racing Team – does not give the engine any more power, but it does offer the rider an extra gear ratio to use. That is especially useful when climbing mountains on an underpowered and over-loaded Indian shopping vehicle.

It would be untrue to say that the birth of Rimini Lambretta Centre's Cyclone gearbox was an easy matter. After months of testing and honing prototype versions, which performed perfectly, Dean took the plunge and invested a massive amount of money in a large production run. Sadly the quality of this batch was not up to the standard of the prototypes, and failures of some gear cogs started to appear. Dean then spent the months leading up to our journey working with the manufacturers to come up with a solution to the failures – which required an exchange component – and then conducting a world-wide product recall on over 100 gearboxes. Individually explaining to over 100 customers why they had to take their gearbox out, and miss some of the best riding weather of the summer, while they waited for a replacement took its toll. Dean was fighting all hours to save both his business and the reputation of an innovative product. He continued to do so right up until the day we left.

When Dean said that he needed this holiday, I knew for certain that he really meant it.

# KIT AND CABOODLE

Irish people – as a rule – are not built for the heat, in much the same way that hippos are not built for Limbo dancing. Tracy has Irish blood in her veins and this substance appears to have a very low ignition point. Like any firework it is best to store Tracy in cool, dark conditions but once lit, do not to return to source of ignition until you are certain that all the explosions are over.

In order to avoid any incendiary episodes riding in the August heat, I thought it wise to take special precautions. Our trio obtained special hot weather motorcycle jackets and gloves from Weise (for the lads) and Tucano Urbano (for Tracy). The jackets include all the usual back, shoulder and elbow armour, but also had mesh ventilation panels in the torso and sleeves to allow for air flow over the body. It really is a liberating experience to feel a rush of wind over your skin like riding in a t-shirt, while at the same time having the confidence of some crash protection.

When it comes to helmets however, we don't do open-face. Both Tracy and I put our faith in the ventilation systems our usual Shoei full-face helmets to allow airflow over the head when moving.

What we couldn't get in ventilated versions were abrasion-resistant trousers, so instead we elected to endure the heat and ride every day in Draggin' and Drayko Kevlar-lined jeans for security. In stretch-fit denim they are more comfortable than normal jeans, and certainly better than the alternative options of leather or synthetic trousers in 40-degree temperatures. Nobody wants boil-in-the-bag genitals.

Typically, Dean and Kim weren't fully suited and booted when we arrived in Italy; which meant a last minute expedition to Mariani Team's motorcycle shop in Forli. The 30km run also afforded Sam and I the opportunity to take the Maico for a final test ride in the heat of a Mediterranean summer.

One problem with squeezing a big engine under the Maico's enclosed bodywork was the build-up of heat radiating from the bespoke 'Custom Chrome' exhaust pipe. The bulbous bodywork may be vented with louvers and large aluminium port-holes, but even with the stainless steel exhaust wrapped in insulation material, the paintwork near your ankles became so hot that it would blister bare skin. At tick-over in traffic the temperature of the seat increased rapidly. Maybe boil-in-the-bag nether regions would be inevitable for Tracy?

At this late stage the only potential solutions were to drill a series of extra holes in the bodywork, or adopt the simple workaround of turning the engine off whenever the scooter was at a standstill. Tracy chose the latter, with tin-ware trepanning held as an option for emergencies.

Dean and Kimberly not only bought new vented jackets and helmets, but also splashed out on a Bluetooth helmet-to-helmet intercom system, much like our borrowed Interphone set. Sadly Interphone's basic version is unable to handle communication between more than two units, meaning that Sam would have to do without.

The intercoms meant that my wife now had a permanent nagging conduit straight to my ear all the time we were riding. I wondered if I'd enjoy this new-found ability to communicate from bike to bike, or whether I'd end up pining for those simpler times when riding a scooter meant the freedom to be alone with your own thoughts.

On the positive side, my wife's conversation now had an 'off' button. Some men would argue that such a control should have been a standard fitment on women from the outset. Tracy would counter this by stating that I'd been doing my best to turn her off for years anyway...

*Route Map*

# EASING INTO THE SWING
## Day 1: Borghi (Italy) To Udine

With the van safely stowed at Rimini Lambretta Centre we were almost ready to go. Marco and Micky were given a set of keys in case we needed any parts posting to us from the stock of used Honda and Suzuki engine spares I'd left in the back.

In my experience it is easy to go crazy packing spare parts for every eventuality, only to end up with a scooter so overloaded that the additional weight actually causes it to fail. Of course the odds are always that the part you break will be the one thing you've forgotten to bring. All you can do is take precautions.

Many years of scooter rally excesses have pickled my brain to the point where my long term memory is useless and my short term one is…

What was I just on about?

My only solution is to write lists and constantly interrogate my poorly-meshed brain cells to figure out if there is anything I've forgotten. Apart from some photocopied duplicates of our documents which I'd left at home, I hoped we were good to go.

One motorcycle touring web forum suggested taking three sets of duplicates in case you need to hand some to police or other drivers in the event of an accident. I wondered how many accidents these bikers planned on having?

An ambitious 7a.m departure hour was chosen in order to avoid the incredible heat of the day. Typically, this drifted nearer to 9a.m before we finally left Borghi.

I'd made allowances to our schedule for 'Italian time' – which is not quite as vague or distant as Spanish 'mañana' – but it's not particularly prompt either. It must have been frustrating in World War II for the religiously punctual Germans to join forces with the Latin countries, for whom 'time' was a far more fluid concept. You only have to look at a Salvador Dali painting to appreciate the flexibility of Spanish time.

Our route took us north up the Adriatic coast road towards Venice, before peeling away from the sea and heading inland towards the medieval city of Udine. While all the scooters behaved perfectly I still endured some technical traumas. The 12-volt power lead from the scooter to my Garmin Sat Nav decided to withdraw from gainful employment. Furthermore, it resigned just as we were required to take a diversion to avoid an accident.

As usual I'd 'cheaped-out' on the Sat Nav. Dedicated motorcycle systems are available for several hundred pounds which offer audio guidance by Bluetooth earpiece. Instead I'd bought a used Garmin car system for £50, which I located around the handlebars in a home-made elasticated pouch. This was a tried, trusted and fundamentally economical method, which had never let me down before. Now it was failing to deliver just when we needed it most.

I'm a technophile at heart so I had a couple of options to call up from the subs bench before I'd resort to buying a paper map. Not only did my Samsung smartphone have access to Google Maps, but my tank bag also contained one of Google's excellent Nexus 7 tablets running a free off-line navigation app called OSMAnd+. With more computing power in my pocket than would have fitted in a school sports hall in the 1970s, I was determined that we would find our way to the Hotel in Udine without resorting to anything as primitive as print.

We did.

Not only was this first day a deliberately short stint in order to ease everyone into the riding routine, but it also terminated in Udine's rather fine Ambassador Palace Hotel; which boasted secure underground parking for the scooters. Here I would introduce Dean to something I learned from long distance Lambretta tourist and former military driver Dean Jordan. This was the very sensible concept of the 'nut & bolt check'.

If the name is not sufficiently self explanatory, it simply means going around the whole bike with sockets and spanners to find out what has started to come loose, and to tighten it before bits fall off completely.

You'd expect the first nut & bolt check to be the one that reveals problem areas on any newly-built machine. Sure enough that turned out to be the case. While my well-used Lambretta appeared to be relatively cohesive, Tracy's Maico was another story. When I checked tightness of vital fasteners – like the single bolt supporting the silencer and the wheel nuts – they had all come loose. This is the problem with having parts powder coated; as we had with the Maico's frame and wheels. While the plastic finish is extremely durable, the coating tends to sag the first time anything is tightened against it, particularly on wheel rims. Having wheels fall off is an inconvenience at best, so Mr Jordan's tip had already proved its worth.

While my tools were scattered around the floor of the underground garage Dean checked the tightness of his wheel nuts and the locking ring on his back hub. As far as I am aware it was the first and last time he used any tools on his scooter for the whole trip. Then again, building scooters correctly is his job…

While topping up my scooter's oil tank with Putoline 2-stroke oil from the five-litre can that rested on the floor boards, I heard a familiar Leicestershire accent. A middle-aged couple were looking at the number plates and trying to figure out if the scooters were from Britain. I felt awkward explaining that we'd only ridden them up from Rimini so far, but the ambition of our destination seemed impressive enough and they wished us all good luck. The British people that you meet in foreign climes are always so friendly. Much friendlier than when you have to live in the same street as the grumpy buggers.

*Locked and loaded at Rimini Lambretta Centre.*

*Udine: the first of many nut & bolt checks. (Photo: Kim)*

# BURNING DESIRE
## Day 2: Udine (Italy) To Leutschach (Austria)

The helicopter that rose up next to our mountainside road from the valley below startled me, but at least it explained what the hell was going on.

In the morning we'd left Udine slightly behind schedule after stopping to buy a new Sat Nav power cable from a large out of town electronics store. This one was expensive but it was also genuine Garmin, so I hoped it would last more than five minutes. By mid-morning the temperature was already over 30 degrees Celsius, but as we climbed into the mountains on our way to the Austrian border we became enveloped in a bank of fog. It felt like riding into a sauna, but how could it be misty when the air is so hot, I wondered?

As the wonderful SS13 road snaked alongside the valley of the River Fella it dawned on me that this was not fog but smoke. Somewhere, out of sight, one of the mountains was on fire. The helicopter that hovered up from the valley bellow had been sucking up the chill mountain water with a massive dangly hose that would make any porn star feel inadequate. Above us another helicopter disappeared over the craggy peaks with a huge tarpaulin bucket full of river water to douse the fire. I admired the skill of these pilots, flying in three dimensions and hovering while their cargo load changes massively in a matter of seconds. Top job.

Pressing on for the Austrian border near Tarvisio, you couldn't help but notice that the Italians who live in this area – the Friuli – behaved more like Austrians or Swiss. Crews pick up litter from the roadside and the area looks spic, span and typically Alpine. Not all of Italy is this tidy.

We stopped for photos at Austria's abandoned border post. Travelling through Europe has become a simple process since the Schengen Agreement of 1995. This freedom of movement is one of few tangible advantages to the whole European Union mess. Sam will never know the trauma that it was to ride across Europe with stops at every border, and a constant need to keep buying and changing local currencies. Actually that's not true, because we still had Turkey to get through, and they remain outside the EU despite a keenness to join. When you see the state of the Greek economy, maybe they should count their blessings.

Our chosen route to Romania via Austria, rather than cutting straight across Slovenia, was at my request, mostly for reasons of nostalgia. I'd previously ridden this celebrated motorcycling road along Austria's southern border on the way to the 2005 EuroLambretta rally. That edition of the rally – which is hosted by a different country each year – was held in a biker campsite called Route 69. I remembered the site having massive beer barrels converted into cabins and imagined it could be fun for us to rent them for the night. I tried to put to the back of my mind that these were, in reality, simply oddly-shaped sheds in which drunken bikers would have spent the subsequent eight years puking and farting, and were presently being baked in 30-degree heat.

After almost 200km of sweating like a fat kid climbing stairs, we passed a swimming lake near Sittersdorf which was just too tempting to miss. It only cost 3 Euros per person to access the Sonnegger See: a small well-kept lake which is bordered by changing rooms, toilets and restaurants. This is as close as land-locked Austrians get to a seaside resort; catering to humanity's ingrained lusts for sunshine and water. Within seconds Sam and Kimberly have torn their swimming costumes from the luggage and bombed into the lake. We spent several hours at the Sonnegger See; which was extremely relaxing, but still left us with many miles to travel.

In the late afternoon our journey resumed on the 'Southern Styria Loop'; a scenic touring route which runs around the south of Austria and northern Slovenia. You could tell how important bikers are to the local economy by the massive stainless steel sculpture of a happy couple riding a motorcycle erected in the middle of one roundabout. The route was also peppered with less festive markers to the same activity. It was impossible to miss the memorials to bikers who didn't make a particular corner; sometimes with a buckled wheel or bent forks used alongside a framed photograph to mark the spot of their demise. Besides acting as tributes to lost friends and family, the intention was obviously to make other riders slow down and consider their own mortality.

In my youth I was so confident in my riding skill that I believed that such a thing would never happen to me, but as I get older this arrogance starts to fade. My reaction time is slower so I need the practice. Only through long journeys and hours in the saddle do you become attuned to the subtle sights and sensations that can save your life. Nobody can predict the future, but you can alter the time it takes in milliseconds for what happens NOW to be processed by your brain and sent as correct instructions to your limbs. If you don't ride far or often then you will become rusty and this process will be too slow or result in the wrong actions being taken.

What many people fail to realise is that for any given speed, riding a scooter is considerably more difficult than riding a motorcycle. A bike's larger diameter wheels and better suspension mean that a motorcyclist can worry less about the road surface, leaving them free to concentrate on taking smooth lines. By contrast, a small-wheeled scooter is highly sensitive to road undulations, drain covers and pot-holes. Avoiding these adds an extra dimension; particularly to cornering and braking. As a result scooter riding is more mentally demanding and tiring, but it is also more involving. The thrill of 'riding on the edge' is equally present, but with a scooter you encounter this 'edge' at lower speeds.

Soon we were climbing the massive Soboth Pass between Lavamund and Eibiswald. With steep, twisty inclines of perfectly surfaced tarmac stretching for miles, Dean's over-laden 186cc engine had to work hard, often flat out in first and second gear. Standard practice on such climbs was for Dean to wave me and Tracy ahead. I tried not to ride too fast because I didn't want to leave him far behind or corner faster than Tracy was comfortable on the hulking Maico.

Half way up the mountain my water-cooled Honda engine started to overheat. It normally runs at 65C but suddenly it had moved beyond 100C because I'd been riding gently using low revs. At such reduced speeds insufficient air is forced through the radiator by my toes. Instead I discovered that the best way to cool it was to ride faster up the mountain and rev the engine more, forcing the water pump to do its job of circulating the coolant. This was the first time that thrashing my scooter was ever the solution to a mechanical issue.

Once over the 1,300-metre crest of the Soboth Pass and following Dean at our regulation 57mph, we were passed by a trio of Austrian bikers on BMWs. I decided to tag onto the back of them for a little fun, dropping a couple of gears to quickly get up to their speed. These were not crazy superbike riders but owners of middleweight touring bikes that were being ridden competently, but far below their limits. If riding solo I'd have delighted in overtaking them mid-corner. However, but with a passenger and luggage this was not the time or place. Instead I settled for blasting past on the straight, down a large hill. Sam made a point of resting his elbow on the bags strapped to the rear of the scooter and looking nonchalantly towards them when we overtook, as if all this was perfectly normal. The bikers took being burned-off by an old Lambretta in good spirits, or at least the third one did as he gave us a thumbs-up when we pulled over to wait for the others. Racing bikes may be immature, but it keeps you young at heart.

As we approached Leutschach I recognised a village where the Austrian police had stopped us in 2005. I was riding a Lambretta chopper at the time and I'd pulled up a few miles earlier to find out if Sam – who was then aged three– wanted to get out of the following van, and ride pillion with me for the last few miles to the campsite. Of course he did.

The authorities rarely shared my enthusiasm for that chopper. Once an angry Dutch policeman told me that the massively extended forks were 'not possible'. I disagreed; they quite clearly were possible because they were holding my front wheel on. What he actually meant was that building such an extreme vehicle would not be legal in Holland. I was perfectly aware of that, but the fact remained that I was English, and my chopper scooter was fully road legal in Britain. Therefore as an EU citizen I was perfectly entitled to ride my abomination in his country, unless it failed to meet a specific rule of the highway, which it didn't.

The Dutch are a funny bunch, as we well knew because our scooter club organised a rally in Holland for over a decade. Their government impose insanely conservative motoring laws that restrict perfectly harmless vehicle modifications, but at the same time they have very liberal views on soft drugs and the sex industry. Let's face it; tourists don't go there for the skiing.

Back in 2005, when I wrestled the long chopper around this particular corner, I was confronted by an Austrian policeman waving me into a lay-by with an extra-large reflective lollipop.

'Do you know the speed limit in that village?' he asked, after checking my passport.

'No, sorry I didn't see the sign', I replied honestly.

'It is 50 kilometres per hour and you were riding at 70 kilometres.'

'Oh, sorry', I replied, expecting the next questions to be about the fact I was riding a chopper made from two Lambretta frames welded together, with huge chromed forks.

'How old is your son?' asked the Austrian copper.

Sam looked up at him from the pillion seat wondering what was wrong.

'He is three. He'll be four in August'

'What is the age that children can ride on the back of a motorcycle in England?' asked the policeman.

'There isn't one', I replied truthfully. 'In Britain the only regulation is that their feet must touch the footpegs and I've moved them so he can comfortably reach them.'

'In Austria children must be 12 before they can ride on the back of a motorcycle.'

'Shall I put him back in the van then?'

'It would be a good idea,' said the policeman, helpfully, before letting us go and then finding another speeder to pull over.

Sam, despite protests, was duly put back in the passenger seat of the van for another few miles before we stopped again and allowed him to reclaim his rightful seat, just in time to ride pillion onto the campsite for his first ever scooter rally.

Eight years and one month later we pulled back onto the Route 69 Biker campsite, again on a Lambretta, and Sam – already taller than his mother – still wasn't legally old enough to ride on the back. Not for another few days at least.

The wooden building that acts as the Route 69 restaurant and bar was sparsely occupied by a few fat, old bikers when we pulled up. There was no welcome for scooter riders and the terse-looking waitress made a point of ignoring us when we sat down at an outside table. I wandered inside to order some drinks and check out the trophy wall to see if my object d'art was still on display.

At the rally in 2005 Tracy and I took it in turns to stay in the tent with Sam at night. She partied on Friday with Lambretta riding chums from all over Europe, which turned out to be a raucous affair lasting until daylight. My turn on Saturday night was far more subdued because many of our European Lambretta chums were now nursing hang-overs. After the gala dinner, members of the London Lambretta Club pointed out burn-marks on the wooden floor of the bar where the campsite owner had performed tyre-smoking burnouts on his motorcycle.

I can't remember exactly why, but some time in the early hours I finally relented to Steve Bone's constant nagging to 'go and get your scooter'.

I went to get my scooter.

The campsite owner didn't bat an eyelid when I rode the chopper into the do, propped the front wheel against the bar, and with the engine screaming like a toddler's tantrum, dumped the clutch.

There are differing opinions about how entertaining this event was, but probably the most unbiased version is a video by the Derby lads that can still be found on the internet. The tuned engine was plenty powerful enough to spin its wheel on the wooden floor and soon filled the entire bar with acrid white smoke. In the video you can hear the bar owner amongst the crowd encouraging me to carry on until the tyre bursts. The thing with 10-inch scooter tyres is that they only have a small contact patch, so by the time I've popped my well-worn Bridgestone, to rousing cheers, the tyre had eaten down through the floorboards by several centimetres.

While most rally-goers seemed to find the burnout entertaining, there were definitely those who didn't. Kev Walsh – then head of the Lambretta Club of Great Britain – was incensed at the time, and highly critical of the burnout in the club magazine Jetset.

I'm pleased to say that the tyre – which we presented to the bar owner the following morning – is still up on the wall, complete with its plaque which reads: 'EuroLambretta 2005 – The deepest hole in the floor'. The ankle injury inducing furrow has since been made safe by filling it with epoxy resin.

Upon our return the campsite was still owned by the same guy, and he recalled that night. In the intervening period his wife had left him, business had been pretty slack and the owner of the barrel-cabins had taken them back. We only had to look around the tables at the age of his patrons – mostly aged over 50 – to see why. The black leather jacket type Biker, like the Scooterboy, is a lifestyle from a moment in time. With more old bikers swapping handlebars for walking sticks than new ones replacing them, his is a scene riding slowly towards extinction.

With no barrels to sleep in we declined his offer to rent rooms in a nearby apartment for 35 Euros a head and instead headed for Leutschach town. For only a little more money we got a 4-star hotel with a restaurant. They even allowed us to push the scooters through the lobby so they could be kept near to our rooms. Try that in London.

*A fire-fighting helicopter sucks water from the River Fella.*
*(Photo: Sam)*

*Massive motorcycle statue in the centre of a roundabout, Austria.*
*(Photo: Sam)*

*Outside the Wankerhof with my chopper: Austria in 2005.
(Photo: Tracy)*

*Burned-out tyre from my chopper, still on the Route 69 biker
campsite wall eight years later.*

# THREE MEALS IN THREE DIFFERENT COUNTRIES
## Day 3: Leutschach (Austria) To Balatonboglar (Hungary)

Another day, another nut & bolt check. This one was particularly fortuitous because we discovered that Tracy's exhaust had snapped. The stainless steel muffler I'd used originally hailed from a modern Triumph triple and its inlet pipe had cracked all the way around. Oh dear. Despite getting up early we weren't going anywhere like that.

Over breakfast the hotelier suggested that we may be able to get it welded at the Renault garage over the road. I duly wandered over at 9a.m to find the showroom staff having their first cup of coffee of the day. Prepared for the fact that they might not speak English, I'd already armed myself with the German word for welding ('schweissen' in case you are interested) using Google Translate on my tablet. I explained that I had 'ein krank auspuff', which literally means 'one sick exhaust'. My attempts at German were clearly amusing, but also comprehensible. The garage owner agreed to do the welding if I brought the scooter round and took the muffler off for him.

By luck this was more than an ordinary Renault dealership owned by an Austrian Arthur Daley. Posters around Autohaus Plasch suggested that they'd previously run a rally car team. Any involvement in motorsports usually signals a competent and well-equipped workshop.

The young mechanics in the yard eyed me suspiciously as I removed the Maicoletta exhaust. However, once the owner realised that the exhaust was made from stainless steel ('edelstahl') he backed out of welding it. Instead he offered to take it to a friend who had equipment more suitable for this tricky material. With that he jumped in his car and reassured me that he would be back in an hour.

By the time we'd packed everything onto the other scooters and checked out of the hotel, I returned to the garage to find the nicely-welded muffler sat on the floorboards. If Mr Plasch had asked for 50 Euros I wouldn't have argued, because the repair got us out of a massive hole, but the bill was only 10 Euros. Problems aren't usually sorted this quickly unless the A-Team are involved. Maybe that's who he got to do the welding?

We were on the road again: next stop Slovenia.

We only had to cross 50km of Slovenia to get to Hungary so I almost feel a cheat to pass comment on the place. This country is northernmost of Tito's former Yugoslavian states. Geographically that put Slovenia in a prime position to conduct trade with Western Europe and avoid the violence that dogged the other Yugoslavian regions following the fall of communism.

The only town on our route is Murska Sobota which appears to have suffered like many others from the degenerative effects of the motorway. The lady who lives inside my Sat Nav and I had a strong difference of opinion about the best way to cross Slovenia. I was intent on adhering to Dean's preference for the minor roads, while she did her best to send us on the motorway. In the end she was probably right.

By the time we found our way onto the old road to Hungary we needed both petrol and food. Typically the arrival of the autobahn meant that anywhere selling such necessities had long since closed down. The best we could manage were some drinks in an odd bar that looked and felt suspiciously like a brothel. The, er, waitress made it clear that to get food or petrol we'd have to go back to town. I absolutely hate having to re-trace our steps, but we had no option. After filling up on petrol and a strange meaty pastry from a rudimentary baker's shop, we stubbornly persisted with the minor road in our quest for the border. I will say this for Slovenia though: even the girl in this baker's shop way off the beaten track spoke reasonable English. Try asking for four sausage rolls in Slovene in your local Greggs the Bakers and see how far you get.

It seems hard to believe, but I remember the Dark Ages. That uncivilised era prior to London having a proper ring-road: England before the M25.

In the 1980s when London's massive orbital motorway was under construction, I lived just inside its arc, on the old A21. That ancient road had for centuries been the main route from the capital to the port of Hastings. As a result Polhill, near my home, catered for passing trade with both a pub and a petrol station. Within a year of the motorway opening the petrol station had closed and the pub eventually followed suit. For some communities, building a motorway is like damming a river. A benefit in one way brings a wilting decay elsewhere.

If I knew very little about Slovenia then my knowledge was encyclopaedic compared to that regarding Hungary:

- *Hungary was part of the Austro-Hungarian Empire before the World Wars.*
- *After WWII it became a communist state.*
- *Hungary was in the way if we wanted to go to Romania.*
- *Hungarians eat goulash.*

To be honest that wasn't the full extent of my knowledge. As soon as Dean mentioned that our route passed Lake Balaton we looked it up to see what was there and find somewhere to stay.

Balaton is basically Hungary's entire compliment of seaside resorts dotted around a single 77km long, shallow lake. I used the hotel Wi-Fi in Austria to book rooms at a place called Simply Szallo, in the small resort town of Balatonboglar. I would claim at the time that I chose this establishment because it meant seeing more of the real Hungary, but it reality I picked it because it was cheap. I overlooked the fact that it only had a 6.1 satisfaction rating on Booking.com.

My rating of Simply Szallo would be; simply don't bother. The 'hotel' consisted of a few rented rooms on the upper storey of a large residential house 400 metres from the lake. To access the lake you had to cross both a main road and a railway line.

Dean and Kimberly's faces dropped when they saw Simply Szallo. There wasn't a straight wall in the place, no air conditioning and the shared showers and toilets appeared to be experiments in bacterial micro-biology.

As soon as we opened a window our room filled with a fog of tiny mosquitoes which enthusiastically flew laps of the low energy light bulb like orbiting satellites. Tracy turned the room into an insect Auschwitz with liberal application of anti-bug spray and we had to shake their tiny bodies off the bedding.

A glance over the balcony revealed that four yobby-looking Austrian lads had commandeered the garden – the aesthetic highlight of Szallo's web gallery – and were swigging beer from cans while bass-heavy music blared from their cabin.

I made a mental note never to stay anywhere again with 'bog' in its name. I should have learned my lesson with Bognor Regis. It could well be twinned with Balatonboglar.

We had no choice but to make the best of it, so we took the kids over the railway line to the lake, which was fantastic. The lakeside was beautifully grassed with steps into the water, which was as warm as a bath. The whole area was spotlessly tidy and all the locals took their litter home with them.

It was clear that the kids loved the lake and wanted to stay longer, but nobody loved Simply Szallo. We resolved to find somewhere better the following day.

That night Tracy didn't fancy riding, so our short trip to a nearby pizzeria was made three-up on the amply long seat of the Maicoletta. I'm not entirely sure what the legal status of riding with three people on one scooter is in the UK, let alone in Hungary. We were all wearing helmets, each of us had sufficient saddle and footrest, and we all remained sober. Instead of worrying about it, I hoped that any traffic police we encountered would have an inbuilt 'too much paperwork' filter, which would render us invisible. Note that this cloaking device is never guaranteed effective, least of all in countries where they can hand out on-the-spot fines.

*Day three: snapped Maico exhaust muffler.*

*One hour later: sorted!*

*Dean pushes the broken Maico through the hotel in Leutschach, Austria.*

*Three-up into town for dinner, Balatonboglar, Hungary. (Photo: Kim)*

# LEAVING THE BOG
## Day 4: Balatonboglar (Hungary) To Siofok

In shame I suggested that Kimberly might do better at choosing the next hotel, which she did using Simply Shitehole Wi-Fi. Her selection was 40km further up the lake, in a major resort town called Siofok.

The Magistern was the tallest hotel in the area. Its imposing grey form reminded me of the soul-sucking housing estate in Thamesmead, South London where they filmed Stanley Kubrick's Clockwork Orange. Once inside, however, things looked up. We were given a suite at the end of the 8th floor with a central living room overlooking the lake, and a large bedroom on each side with a balcony. In any Western country this suite would be extortionately expensive in August, but for us it was pretty reasonable so we booked an additional night straight away.

The Magistern represented everything about holidays that would give me nightmares if I was trapped there for a week. Retired people and families with young kids dominated the place, eating the same full-board buffet (which was actually very good) night after night and watching demonstrations of Hungarian traditional dancing for the disinterested tourists. I suspected that the two girls who whooped along with the tunes would make great prostitutes given such expertise at faking enthusiasm for their partner's moves. The hotel was just a world of holiday normality, and Lake Balaton could easily be swapped for the Costa del Sol.

I liked the Hungarians though – they seemed tidy and polite – helping old people and kids on the steps into the lake, rather than impatiently barging through like Italians sometimes do. The population also seemed healthier than the Brits – there were a few obese people around but at least they were tanned fatties. By contrast the locals had to endure our ghost-like bodies slathered in liberal dousings of Sun Factor Dufflecoat.

The nearest swinging entertainment was only a short ride away in

Siofok town centre. There we descended into a full-on Chav environment, like Ibiza Town, Blackpool or Rimini, complete with snake handlers, beefcake blokes, barely-dressed beauties and boys with black eyes. Every coastline has a place like this for the 'yoof' to let off steam, and Lake Balaton's extensive shoreline is no exception.

The two big local night-clubs touted for business in interesting ways: Palace, which hosts big name international dance DJ's, flew banners down the beach behind a decrepit looking communist-era propeller plane. Meanwhile Flört Club used a rather amusing poster featuring Italy's prize political plum Silvio Berlusconi, to promote their 'Bunga Bunga' party. It speaks volumes about his international reputation that even the Hungarians find him funny.

In Siofok we quickly fell into beach holiday mode: swimming, karting and generally letting the kids have fun. The only fly in my soup was the loss of my Canon compact camera on the busy beach. I soon bought another compact camera for the remaining journey, but the photos from the first few days remain irreplaceable.

*Vespa 50 Special outside an Italian restaurant in Siofok.*

*Poster for Flört club's Bunga Bunga night, Siofok, Hungary.*

# ARE YOU FEELING HUNGARY?
## Day 6: Siofok to Mako

At around midnight on our second night in the Magistern, an intense electrical storm threatened to put an end to the stifling heat wave. A ferocious wind swept the lake into a boiling frenzy, with waves splashing onto the shoreline. Items of our clothing – which we'd left drying on the balcony – were redistributed across the hotel lawn by the storm. I ran down to try in vain to photograph some of the lightning strikes hitting the far side of the lake, only to hear the ecstatic shrieks of a young couple swimming just off the shore and enjoying the agitated water.

I never did find my swimming trunks.

The storm was all bluster. By the morning it still hadn't rained, but the titanium sky looked swollen with rain, so we packed up to head for Mako near the Romanian border. Or rather we waited, while Dean laboriously wrapped all his clothes bags in bin liners. In terms of providing a perfect rainproof seal in arduous conditions this is about as effective as putting a condom on a cactus. There's a lot to be said for the yellow roll-top bags that Tracy and I bought for few quid from Aldi. They are inherently waterproof and save all that messing about with plastic bags.

The journey began quite shakily: dodging box-dropping lorries and a car crash caused by smoke from a burning field alongside the road. The day continued in the same vein with our first terrible tarmac of the trip. It was as if the road had been laid by workers more adept at laying roof tiles.

My lack of historical knowledge about Hungary was soon corrected by the chance sighting of a museum near Kiskunmajsa dedicated to the 1956 uprising. This was when the Hungarians fought against Soviet occupation, which had been imposed at the end of World War II.

I'd first seen signs for the museum while having my teeth rattled out on the rough back road. In the end it was fairly easy to spot, thanks to the Russian T55 tank parked in the garden of what was once a tiny local school situated in the middle of nowhere.

After glancing at the un-mown lawns and dishevelled building, the '56-os Museum looked suspiciously closed. I suspected that a photo opportunity of the scooters in front of a tank was the best we'd get. Thankfully that wasn't the case. As if by magic a rather lovely young female curator appeared, like a sexy version of the shop keeper from Mr Benn.

She explained that following the World War II occupation of Hungary, Russia spent the next decade extracting war reparations from the former Axis state, aided and abetted by a puppet communist government.

On 23rd of October 1956 a demonstration by 200,000 people in Budapest against the regime ended in bloodshed when students attempted to enter the national radio building with a list of demands. The hard-line Hungarian AVH state police fired on the crowd, killing many before they were overcome. Members of the Hungarian army joined the rebellion, attacking both the AVH and Soviet troops. Soon the rebellion spread across the entire country and the Soviet-controlled government was toppled. People celebrated by cutting the communist symbol from the centre of the Hungarian flag.

The Soviet Union had recently seen Nikita Khrushchev handed the reins following the death of Stalin. Khrushchev's initial response to the uprising was to waver, withdrawing Russian troops to a safe distance and offering to negotiate with the fledgling government. Then, after a warning from China that any perceived weakness could create a domino effect in communist Europe, Khrushchev changed his mind. On the 4th of November the Politburo sent the might of the Soviet military to crush the Hungarian uprising.

The museum is dedicated to the 5,500 Hungarians killed in the rebellion, many of whom were poorly-armed civilian militia standing up to the tanks of the Soviet army. One tactic used by the rebels was to leave upturned metal soup dishes in the road to fool Russian tank commanders into thinking they were land-mines.

In the end the battle was hopelessly uneven. 200,000 Hungarians fled over the Austrian border before the Soviets sealed it and installed another satellite regime, which governed Hungary until the fall of communism in 1989.

The museum was established by Pongrátz Gergely, who commanded a group of rebels that successfully destroyed as many as 12 Russian tanks in Budapest with little more than Molotov cocktails. He lived in exile in USA until 1991, when he returned to set up the museum and chapel as a memorial to those who fought to free their country. If the rebellion had succeeded in kicking the communists out of Hungary in 1956, then central Europe might have been a very different place. Instead the Iron Curtain remained tightly drawn for another 33 years.

What bothered me most about our tour was that such a pretty and intelligent young girl should be left alone to run the slightly decrepit museum. Still, with rooms full of Kalashnikovs, I suppose she had enough firepower to look after herself in the event of trouble.

Given how pleased most Hungarians are to have finally escaped the oppression of communism, it seemed odd to find people in our next stop of Szeged dabbling with soviet-era nostalgia.

Szeged is a beautiful historic university town, and we rode into the main square during the self-congratulatory 'I love Szeged' festival. This not only consisted of a medieval market, but also a vintage vehicle meeting. We cheekily rode into the middle of their parade only to be accosted by a reporter with a microphone. After a difficult but mercifully short interview, we parked our scooters with some of the vintage motorcycles and joined in the fun.

In such clean and obviously European surroundings it was initially difficult to see the effects of communism, but the vehicles on display explain perfectly how different the worlds on either side of the Iron Curtain must have been. No vintage fair in Britain or Italy would be complete without a Vespa or Lambretta representing the 1960s, but such clean-cut capitalist devices were not available to the Hungarians. Instead their locally-produced equivalent was called the Csepel Tünde (Elf): a 175cc scooter that I'd never seen in the metal before. It was certainly no Lambretta in the styling stakes, but still better than many of the monstrous scooters conjured up when British manufacturers tried to cash in on the 1950s scooter craze.

The rest of the 'old-timer' display was made up of an oddball selection of vehicles, many of which were two-stroke, including Trabant cars and locally made Pannonia twin-cylinder bikes. Most vehicles were of communist origin but with the odd imported curve-ball thrown. I've seen German WWII motorcycle outfits before, but never a Zündapp KS 750 being driven around the streets by a fat man with his equally portly wife at the trigger of the sidecar-mounted machine gun.

Friendliest of this bunch was not actually a Hungarian. First to approach us was Tomislav Vidakovic, president of the Oldtimer club from Subotica, just over the border in Serbia. As a Vespa owner he took a great interest in our scooters and tried to lure us to a vintage meeting in his home town the following day, even going so far as to organise some accommodation. As far as Dean and I were concerned, following fate was a tempting proposition. However Tracy pragmatically pointed out that Serbia was also in the opposite direction to Istanbul, so we politely declined Tom's offer.

Besides the Oldtimer meeting and the medieval fair, it was also wedding season. An endless stream of brides and grooms queued up to hit the Game Over button in Szeged's grandiose town hall. Each of these ceremonies appeared to be escorted by a chap dressed in traditional Hungarian costume of ridiculous waistcoat and ankle-swinging trousers. They reminded me of mates from the scooter rallies who are obsessed with equally oddball mid-70's skinhead fashion.

In the late afternoon we reluctantly left Szeged when there seemed to be much left worth exploring. After my previous hotel-booking disaster I'd once more been allowed to choose the night's accommodation; this time at Camping Mako in the town of the same name.

I have a theory about travelling which states that: the more stars a hotel displays, the fewer interesting people you are likely to meet.

I've stayed in a few five-star hotels with various jobs and to be frank, I don't really like them. Five stars generally mean being looked down on for dressing as I do, and having bell-boys try to wrestle bags from you in the hope of a tip. If I've got my luggage through the door on my own then I can probably carry it as far as my room, thanks.

The whole ethic of more expensive hotels is about maintaining separation: getting away from the street, getting away from other guests, getting away from anything that might be fun, in a boisterous sense. Of course, where you really meet other interesting travellers is at the other end of the price scale; on campsites and in youth hostels.

On a scooter odyssey in 1989 I met a Japanese hippy girl called Mami in an Athens youth hostel who said she wanted to travel to see friends in England. Without any thought of sexual conquest (Mami reminded me of Yoko Ono and I really didn't fancy her), I offered her a lift to London on the back of my Lambretta chopper, and she accepted. My point being that you'll often struggle to find anyone to talk to in a posh hotel, let alone someone who'd gladly accept a lift for 1,200 miles on the back of a heavily modified scooter.

We'll return to that tale later on…

The thing that puts me off youth hostelling nowadays is that I am no longer a youth. I am a father with some responsibility, so we have to look for a little compromise between comfort and communion. Thankfully Camping Mako proved to be just the ticket.

After crossing a bridge on the road from Szeged, Camping Mako is a sharp U-turn back down to the north bank of the River Maros. Our compromise was to rent impossibly picturesque 3-person bungalows on the campsite, which I had reserved in the laziest manner by sending the owner Istvan an SMS message. Despite having nothing but my UK mobile number he honoured the booking.

Istvan couldn't have been more chilled if he'd been bathed in liquid nitrogen. We were given the keys and told we could park the scooters right outside the bungalows if we liked. There was no hurry for passports or payment, but would we like breakfast in the morning?

The site was beautifully kept and surrounded by orchards and allotments. Squirrels scampered around, making it feel like we'd accidentally ended up in a scene from Bambi. After my previous booking disaster I was extremely relieved to have made a popular choice. I was also impressed that my 'interesting people in budget accommodation' theory was vindicated, for there next to a small slug-shaped tent was a white Vespa PX200 with a Turkish number plate.

Hassan, the owner of the Vespa and a member of the Istanbul Vespa Club, was more than helpful. He owns 25 Vespas in total and does a different tour every summer by scooter. Sadly, he didn't have a lot of good things to say about his home town, certainly from a scooter riding perspective. The traffic, he warned us, is an absolute nightmare, but he offered suggestions on the easiest route into the city. He even gave us the contact details for some scooter shops and his two Vespa-riding sons in case we encountered problems. You couldn't ask for more from someone you'd only met five minutes previously.

*Unstable load, Hungary.*

*Dean and Tracy with a Russian T55 tank at the '56-os Museum, Hungary.*

*Hand-driven medieval merry-go-round, Szeged.*

*Hungarian Csepel Tünde 175 scooter in Szeged.*

*World War II German Zündapp KS750 military sidecar outfit.*

*Turkish Vespa rider Hassan at Camping Mako, Hungary.*

*Our home for the night.*

# CULTURE SHOCK
## Day 7: Mako (Hungary) To Deva (Romania)

Romania's chief export, if you believe the Daily Mail, is Romanians to Britain. Even without reading UK newspapers you'd be hard pushed not to have encountered dire warnings about how the British Isles will be flooded with Romanian and Bulgarian immigrants, as soon as their citizens are given freedom to work anywhere within the EU states in January 2014.

I was keen to see what was so bad about the place that almost 3 million people have left in the last decade, reducing the population to 19 million. Tracy was less keen to enter Romania due to reports from a different source. Dean had already ridden in the country and loved it, but he warned that the road surfaces were terrible. On the last trip his group were told never to ride in the dark due to hidden potholes and stolen drain covers. They subsequently met a pair of motorcyclists in a hotel who had ignored this advice, one of whom now had a buckled wheel and forks bent under his bike after riding into an open drain in the dark.

For the Maicoletta, which has soft front forks that are prone to 'bottoming out', any big pothole could spell disaster. For Tracy, who is a less confident rider, this was a major concern.

The Toth family at Camping Mako equipped us with an amazing breakfast before we navigated the short distance to the Romanian border. After such a warm welcome we were sad to leave Hungary.

'Mama Mia!' remarks the Romanian border guard incredulously, as we tell him that we are riding these vintage scooters to Istanbul. I'm pleased to have shocked someone who regularly sees horse-drawn vehicles on the road. After a quick glance at the passports he waves us through without drama.

At the roadside is a booth selling passes permitting use of Romania's few motorways, but the good news is that motorcyclists don't need them. We press on down the single-lane road into a snaking train of articulated lorries. Almost immediately we see our first horse-drawn cart, which is being checked over by the police. The carts use car wheels offering the ride comfort of pneumatic tyres. Maybe the tyre tread is below the legal limit, if indeed such legislation exists for horse-drawn vehicles? I very much doubt it.

The first few miles do have a relatively decent road surface – certainly no worse than you'll find in Britain – so I remain optimistic that things have improved since Dean's last visit. None of us has any Romanian currency so we elect to stop at the nearest cash-point to withdraw some Lei. The first ATM is at a branch of the Banca Transilvania, in a rough looking neighbourhood. I make a point of looking around the machine for any duplicating devices attached to the card slot. I don't know why but I'm already on my guard, probably through subconsciously absorbed prejudice.

Romania was one of the first countries in the world to switch from paper to plastic for its banknotes, and each note contains a transparent panel which makes it very difficult to forge. The Banca Transilvania cash machine dispenses notes like Sesame Street's Count Who Loves to Count:

'One ah ah. Two ah ah...'

No, not really.

At least so far the roads aren't too bad, and we've got a good guide. On Dean's last tour the lads developed a solution for dealing with poor road surfaces, which entails the lead rider swerving around a pothole and immediately dropping a hand to point out its location, thereby allowing the following riders to take evasive action. It is a system that works very well as long as you don't ride too close together, and the speeds are low enough that there is time to react. However this information is only useful if you have somewhere to go, which is not always the case.

As Dean's scooter skips into the air I see his hand drop to point out what is effectively a tarmac lump the height of a kerb running across most of the road, but Tracy has no possibility to avoid it and hits the rut at 55mph. With insufficient suspension travel to cope with such a jolt, her scooter leaves the ground and Tracy momentarily leaves saddle. The heavy Maico crashes back to earth after its brief flight. Thankfully she manages to regain control. Via the intercom, my ears are now filled with blue language which makes it abundantly clear that Tracy's initial opinion of Romania is lower than a mole's underpants.

I try to retain an open mind, but if I'm honest compared to tidy Hungary this place is literally a dump, with rubbish strewn everywhere. It only gets worse as we approach the city of Arad, which Dean has warned us is 'a bit of a shit-hole'.

He's not kidding. As we skirt around the city centre the flowing traffic regularly comes to an almost complete standstill, before picking up speed again. The problem is the railway tracks, which cross the road without so much as a barrier; only lights that flash when a train is coming.

Road engineers in most countries have solved the rail crossing conundrum by ensuring that the road is at the same height as the railway track wherever the two intersect. Not in Arad they haven't.

Here the tracks tended to be 10cm higher or lower than road surface, causing bumps that reduce even 4-wheel-drive cars to walking pace. On the scooters we cross extremely slowly with our feet down, taking care not to scrape our vulnerable exhaust systems.

Such is the speed reduction at these railway crossings that groups of beggars roam the road in hope of a hand-out from delayed motorists. At one crossing we are approached by a decrepit woman pushing a fellow with no lower legs in a wheelchair. This reminds me of the scene in Toy Story where Buzz and Woody are accosted by all the mutant toys. Maybe, like in the cartoon, the freaks would turn out to be really nice people if we took the time to get to know them.

We aren't hanging about to find out.

I'm afraid that my relationship with beggars has been prejudiced by an encounter I had in the London district of Soho around 1989. A group of us were returning home from a nightclub when a lad not much older than me asked for some spare change. He was sat in a shop doorway under a small, dirty blanket with a puppy. All the smart ones have a puppy. In Britain we are a nation of animal lovers over and above our sympathy for fellow humans.

'Sorry mate', I said routinely, before turning back and saying: 'I don't want to be rude but you look healthy enough, why don't you get a job instead of begging?'

Asking that sort of question is not the done thing in these situations, but he took it well enough.

'Well, what could I do?'

'I work as a courier, delivering parcels on a scooter', I told him. 'You could do that, even if you had to steal a pushbike to get started on.'

'How much could I earn if I was a courier?'

'I don't know, maybe £50 a day.'

'I earn more than that', laughed the beggar.

'Well, if you earn more than me, why the hell should I give you my money?'

I'd heard legends of professional beggars in London who got picked up by a car at the end of their 'shift', but this was a confirmed encounter with the begging elite.

Fair play, it's good to have a career, but his attitude meant that the genuinely needy have had diddly-squat from me ever since: apart from Big Issue sellers, charity shops and the odd donation when there's a natural disaster. I did once give some Rupees to one young lad in Delhi who then took me as a soft touch and pestered me for the rest of my stay. One of us clearly didn't understand the nature of that transaction. As the amateur party, I suspect it was probably me.

I hoped that our Romanian experiences would improve when we stopped for fuel and food; which was thankfully way past Arad. We found a small café and hotel at the rear of the next petrol station, and things looked up a little. Sat at an outside table, overlooking the scooters, Dean was suddenly accosted by the owner, who asked in fluent Italian, if we had ridden from Italy. He recognised Dean's Italian number plate and soon revealed that he'd worked for many years in Bagno 46: one of Rimini's many beach bars. Pretty soon the owner was personally cooking us a meal of breaded chicken and chips, which was plain but good, before rejoining us at the table.

While we ate, a mongrel bitch, with saggy teats that nearly scraped the ground, eyed our lunch with her one remaining eye. Dogs would be a common feature of the Romanian experience.

We learned that this region had previously been part of Hungary until the end of WWI, and that the hotelier's ancestors were actually Hungarian.

One thing that surprised me was the Romanian language. This is Latin-based and quite similar to Italian. Physically though, the two countries are separated by Hungary, which has its own distinct tongue, and the former Yugoslavian states with their Slavic dialects. One thing is for certain: centuries of wars and upheavals have messed up central Europe more than a stray hand grenade rolled into a kid's birthday party.

Between Arad and Deva – our final destination for the day – we made a brief coffee stop in a fairly unfriendly roadside joint. Unfriendly, apart from one fellow customer: a big-cat handler from a circus in Belgium. He was travelling to Constanta on the Romanian coast to discuss an 'animal swap' with some friends from another circus.

'It's not every day you get to meet a lion tamer', I said to Dean as we were leaving.

Dean looked unconvinced, but the guy shouted after us to look at the back of his trailer. Sure enough, in the window were circus posters and photos of the performer with his tigers.

The hotel in Deva was chosen by way of a group decision because I was paranoid about getting it wrong again. Vila Paradis looked brilliant in the photos and had rave reviews on Booking.com. What the reviews and photos failed to reveal was that Paradis is surrounded on every side by 6-storey blocks of ugly, crumbling concrete flats. It is truly a rose between thorns.

We arrived to the sound of a screaming woman chastising someone in a nearby flat. Some fat, sweaty blokes in vests attempted to fix a broken Dacia (an old Renault model built under licence in Romania) by dropping cigarette ash onto the engine. The whole place had the air of a hell-hole council estate in Britain where you couldn't leave any scooter unlocked for more than a few seconds. Not unless you wanted it to be ridden around fields by yobby kids and eventually set on fire.

Unfortunately Vila Paradis had no secure parking. The people who ran the place could sense our misapprehension, and assured us that they'd never had a problem with any motorcycles left parked outside. When we still weren't convinced, the owner offered to put the scooters in one of the hotel's immaculate dining rooms and tore up some cardboard boxes to protect the carpet. That sealed the deal.

After a quick sightseeing ride around the city (flats, flats, litter, flats, amazing building, flats, castle, flats) we ended up parking the scooters outside the front of the hotel all night anyway. We returned hungry, particularly after realising that we'd crossed another time zone in entering Romania. By this stage we were two hours ahead of Greenwich and one hour late for our dinner. Thankfully service in the in-house restaurant was prompt and the meal fantastic.

*Making a withdrawal at the Blood Bank, Romania.*

*Transparent Romanian Lei.*

# MOUNTAIN MAYHEM
## Day 8: Deva (Romania) to Curtea De Arges

Our scooters may not look much to the untrained eye, but to us they are highly valuable, not only as transport, but for the cost in man-hours and parts it took to modify each one. As soon as you put your heart and soul into tailoring something to your personal requirements, and particularly if it has served you well on an adventure such as this, then the scooter becomes more than a mere vehicle. It becomes irreplaceable, like a child. As such I don't think we were being unreasonable in our concern for their security.

In Deva we parked the scooters near to the windows of our rooms, secured with vibration-sensitive Xena alarm locks on the disc brakes. With wire cables linking each bike, moving any one would set off an ear-piercing 120dB siren. Thankfully we didn't hear a peep out of them all night, and the machines were still present and correct when I checked them in the morning.

My reappraisal was that the surrounding apartment blocks may be ugly, but that didn't necessarily make it a bad neighbourhood. It's simply that in Deva blocks of crumbling flats, once given freely by the communist state, are the only homes available to the majority of people.

While strapping our luggage back on I noticed a gypsy woman with a mouth full of gold teeth. She was walking up the hill with a 3-year old lad who was clearly fascinated by the scooters, so I picked him up and sat him on the seat of my Lambretta. He looked a little nervous but his grandma gave me a friendly grin with her mouth like a broken treasure chest. I made a mental note to be less judgemental, which is not easy to do if you've lived in a big city where snap decisions and natural suspicion are tools that ensure your safety.

As we were about to leave the hotel, the female chef who cooked our tasty meals the previous night, tried to drive off in her car, but there was a problem. After a few metres of a slapping noise she realised that one of the tyres was totally flat. However with our engines running and time ticking for a busy day we elected not to help and rode off.

Was this bad karma?

On a road trip the concept of karma as a belief system is probably as good as any of the alternatives. Conversely, any religion that tells believers that they will go to a better place when they die should not be relied upon as a source of careful drivers. Thankfully it is only extremist idiots that are so certain of heaven's bounty that they are willing to strap on a suicide vest, or drive with utter contempt for their own safety. The vast majority of religious folk, despite nominally qualifying for a place in heaven, still look both ways when crossing the road. They might be believers, but they're not 100% convinced about the benefits of the afterlife are they?

On balance I'm not certain about any cosmically-inspired karma either, but the fact is that most people train themselves to spot nice people and are nice to them in return. Or alternatively, the predatory ones simply pounce on them.

Either way, I suffered a pang of guilt for not helping the chef change her wheel, but it would have been a different story if she was alone on an empty road rather than in the middle of a busy housing estate. I felt sure that there would be a fat man in a string vest along to help at any minute.

Romania is slowly being improved: at least in terms of infrastructure. Gradually the main roads – which are often single carriageways passing through ancient town centres – are being bypassed by multi-lane ring-roads. This is probably a good thing, because towns yet to be upgraded seem to be pierced by endless strings of lorries like a gigantic game of KerPlunk. Taking the place of the marble in this scenario, we needed to find the easiest path through these obstructions, which often dictated long periods filtering past on the wrong side of the road.

At least Romania is progressing and traffic will move faster and more freely when the work is completed. By contrast traffic in England seems to move slower year by year, as the overstretched transport networks grind to a halt. Central London has an average daytime traffic speed of 8 mph. That's no faster than when every cab was pulled by a horse.

One of the towns given a new ring-road is Sibiu, and the bypassing traffic left us with a smoother run into the medieval centre. Here, the roofs incorporate unusual windows under arched tiles so that the ancient buildings appear to be watching you. Unable to close these eyes, the houses were forced to witness the horror of their streets being ripped up for the installation of new pipework.

I chuckled as one workman shouted at a digger driver just in time to stop him reversing over a box of brand new components. Silent movie fans can rest easy: Laurel and Hardy are alive and well, and bringing a slapstick twist to road works in Romania.

Ironically our next destination was not a place but a route: the Transfagarasan Highway; acclaimed as the greatest road in the world by the Top Gear crew, despite it being little more than the engineering folly of a tyrant.

It is widely accepted that Romania's former communist leader Nicolae Ceausescu helped put the dick in dictator. After first taking the reins of power in 1967, he then bankrupted the country with a series of ill-conceived schemes until finally he was deposed by a revolution in 1989. Ceausescu was given as little mercy as he had shown to his downtrodden people, and died facing the bullets of a firing squad.

The man is not without his legacies though, including the sinewy Transfagarasan which snakes over a previously impassable section of the Carpathian mountain range. Ceausescu had the road constructed as a way of moving troops north from the capital in the event of a Russian invasion, but it proved to be a massive and dangerous undertaking, consuming 6,000 tons of explosives, costing the lives of over 40 men and taking four years to complete prior to its inauguration in 1974.

Before we can tackle the mountains we must stop in a supermarket on the edge of Sibiu for supplies. Kimberly has officially become a teenager today so our plan is to mark the occasion by holding her birthday party at the top of the Transfagarasan. Quite deliberately the location is the only cool thing about it. The trolley is loaded with balloons, Tom 'N' Jerry party hats and Hello Kitty paper cups to hold the cheapest bubbly wine we can find.

'Scooterist Cheese and Wine parties' in unusual locations have been the surprise hit of 2013's scooter rallies, with the best so far being The Gout Club's afternoon soirée on the Hardknott Pass: Britain's steepest road. It is our ambition to take this latest 'extreme sport' to another level.

While in the shopping centre I also purchased some truly nasty blue and white tablecloth pattern swimming shorts to replace the ones that blew off the balcony in Hungary. I have little choice because these are the only type they sell. The checkout girl even compounds my misery by leaving the security tag on, thus making it look like I stole them…

As we leave Sibiu, the impressive Fagaras Mountains rise up as if sprouting from the plateau we were riding on. Ceausescu may have wanted the Transfagarasan built to quickly shift his tanks if Romania was ever threatened by Russia, but this would only have worked if the Russians decided to attack in the summer. At 2,034 metres high the road is only clear of snow and open to traffic for a few months each year.

Thankfully we remember to fill up with fuel on the main N1 road before turning off towards the pass. A group of Hungarian bikers roll into the petrol station after their descent. They explain that the road surface is not really suitable for sporty riding and moan that despite waiting for 40 minutes to get some good photos, the highest points remained frustratingly enveloped in fog. The bikers also seem quite surprised that we are going over on vintage scooters, but they shut up completely when we say that this is just part of our route to Istanbul.

I'm not being boastful, just telling the truth, but it's wise to remember wherever you travel that there's always someone who has done it earlier, faster or using a more difficult method. Indeed, wherever we've ridden you can guarantee that someone else has cycled or walked in the past.

The Transfagarasan is a bit of a slow burner with the first few miles of switchback climbing done between walls of conifers. Steadily, gaps appear in the trees and you realise how far you've climbed. Suddenly, after several roofed galleries, the famous panorama appears. It's as if someone has taken a spoon and scooped out a section between two ice cream mountains, and then carved in a zigzag path from the bottom to the top with the tip of a fork. It's a hugely impressive sight, particularly as the fog that dogged the Hungarian riders has now vanished into the very thin air.

Tracy and I leave Dean far behind on the long climb. I try to keep a comfortable pace for the Maico, while at the same time getting some air-flow through the radiator and overtaking the odd dawdling Romanian biker.

Our party venue is a large lay-by, where Kimberly attempts to pop the cork on her Romanian 'champagne' only to find that the bottle is a screw-top. The sweet liquid is a perfect accompaniment to local crackers which combine both the taste and texture of cardboard, and some sliced cheese which is strangely reminiscent of trainer insoles.

Romania remains true to form in that this viewing spot of natural beauty and triumphant engineering is littered with cans, plastic cutlery and food wrappers. Unlike the locals, we pack our rubbish away and take it with us.

After the final twists and turns of the climb the road avoids the mountain peak by way of a dark, dank and very windswept tunnel. This delivers us, squinting, onto the greener southern side of the slopes. It's only downhill from here.

Tracy is keen to not to hold anyone up, so she sets off down the mountain ahead. Dean elects to pause for some photos while Kim calms down sufficiently from the giddiness of her party. He also wants to fulfil his promise of letting her ride the scooter on the Transfagarasan, which she does for a few metres in a large, deserted lay-by. This leaves me and Sam to carve down the mountain at a more enthusiastic pace.

Oh shit, this road is steeper than it looks.

The first few kilometres of snaking tarmac require constant use of the brakes to arrest our speed. My scooter has a hydraulic disc brake at each end offering far more stopping power than the primitive standard drum brakes on Dean's Lambretta. However after a few minutes of enthusiastic riding I can smell the pads baking, as the friction surfaces overheat and begin to glaze. A few corners further on and it suddenly takes two frantic steps on the rear brake pedal to illicit any reaction. There's nothing for it but to pull over and strip off the rear brake to inspect for wear. Thankfully it is simply a case of boiled brake fluid, with the doctor's orders being a few minutes cooling down and a dose of less enthusiastic riding. I am surprised that Dean has still not arrived despite our pit-stop, but I don't want to let Tracy get too far ahead, so Sam and I push on after her.

Top Gear's eulogising gave the impression that the Transfagarasan was a billiard-table smooth automotive playground; which is not the case. When riding southwards the surface up to the peak is mostly good, but the road down is sandy, slippery and broken in places. However the biggest hazard we encounter has four legs and a tail. Romania has a massive problem with stray dogs: literally millions are thought to be living on the street. While most individual hounds are well behaved; those in packs can get extremely rowdy. Twice on our descent groups of dogs ran out into the road to chase or attack us. That is a genuinely scary situation on a scooter, because hitting anything larger than a Dachshund would almost certainly cause us to crash. I found the best solution was to aim straight for any packs of aggressive looking dogs, and then to swerve around them at the last minute. If you initially move to the other side of the road to avoid them and they keep coming for you, then you have nowhere left to go.

This south side of the mountains is beautiful. The Alpine tree lines and craggy rock faces are dotted with tents and caravans parked in impossibly odd places. This is free-camping Romanian style and it looks like fun. Bikers crouching around campfires look up as they hear my engine and give a friendly wave, but we can't stop. We've already booked into a hotel just north of the first big town – Curtea de Arges – but now we are running late and dusk is upon us. Progress feels extremely slow as the road relentlessly doubles back on itself along the banks of the Vidraru: the man-made lake created in 1965 by damming the River Arges and so turning the mountain rainfall into free electricity. I'm torn between pressing on to catch Tracy and stopping to change my tinted visor for a clear version. In the end it is too dangerous to carry on as I can longer see the broken surface whenever trees overhang the road. Swapping screens only takes a few seconds on a Shoei helmet, unlike finding the spare visor when it is buried deep inside your luggage. The delay gives Sam a moment to moan about the discomfort of our seat. That seat being the most comfortable Lambretta saddle I could find before the trip and one that we then modified to sit further back on the frame to give us both more space. The fact is that Lambrettas are small and designed for going to the shops, but we are both big and riding across Europe. In terms of leg-room this is the Ryanair of scooters, so a little discomfort is to be expected. At the rate Sam is growing this might be the last long journey we do together on a Lambretta.

It has gone 8.30pm by the time all five of us are reunited just before the Vidraru Dam, and our hotel is still another half hour away. Finding the place, however, presents something of a challenge. The lady in my Sat Nav has gone on strike and the screen shows nothing but a straight line representing the main road. I have the address but everyone in the villages of tiny decrepit looking bungalows seems so drunk that they can barely stand, let alone be able to give directions in a foreign language.

Eventually, near a huge sign of a cartoon fish with 'CRAP FISHING' written underneath, we do find the hotel, but we are not given a warm welcome. The receptionist has to put down her dinner plate long enough to explain in broken English that they have given away one of our booked rooms. Consequently they don't have beds for all of us. The girl calls the hotel owner and passes the phone to Tracy who, like me, is now in fireworks mode. The owner explains that we have missed the last check-in time, but they did try to phone to see if we were still coming. I check my mobile and sure enough I'd missed a call from a Romanian number while we were searching for the hotel.

By this stage night has fallen, so rather than brooding we discuss our options. We can continue to Curtea and hope to find somewhere else, but with Dean's warnings about the dangers of riding at night on bumpy Romanian roads, nobody is keen. Maybe we can all stay here in one room, and those without beds can use the camping mats and sleeping bags? It's not ideal, but it will do as long as we can get something to eat.

The girl looks up from her now cold plate of food and explains that we won't be dining as the kitchen is closed. That seals the deal. Tracy gives her a look that says 'I hope you choke on that' and we are forced to hit the road again.

As we ride slowly and carefully down the unlit country street into Curtea de Arges I wonder if this problem could have been avoided with better karma. Maybe if we'd stopped to help the chef change her wheel in Deva, then things might have been different? Of course they would: we'd have been even later arriving in Curtea.

The next hotel sign we encountered pointed to a place called 'Manole' where the owner proudly showed me a 6-birth dormitory with prison-like bunk beds and no linen. Dean's travel tip for Romania is to always ask to see the rooms before checking in, and I'm glad we did. As he points out; 'Grand, stylish entrances don't mean for one minute that you're going to get a grand, stylish room to sleep in.'

Despite my karmic uncertainty, I didn't think we'd done anything bad enough to deserve a night in prison, so we withdrew from the 'Man Hole' and pushed on again towards the small city centre. There we found a large modern-ish hotel with a restaurant staffed by the winner of 'Romania's Grumpiest Waitresses 1997' awards. It's good to see she was keeping up her skills, but then again she had the support of a strong team.

I declined the option of 'Grilled Crap' from the English menu. It turns out that 'crap' is the Romanian word for 'carp', but there is a world of difference in the position of those middle two letters, particularly when selecting a main course.

*Dean and Kim are a dot on the climb up the Transfagarasan Pass.*

*Kim's 13th birthday party.*

*'It's been emotional'.*

*The local bus, Vidraru.*

*Sam massaging his sore buttocks, Lake Vidraru.*

# THE REAL ROMANIA
## Day 9: Curtea De Arges to Bran

Curtea, when we awoke, was a much prettier place than the little we'd been able to see in the dark. Tracy discovered that the street outside the hotel was now lined with market stalls selling all manner of touristy tat, but what were the tourists here to see?

The answer, a few hundred metres ahead past the market, was the fantastic 16th century Curtea de Arges Cathedral: a glowing Byzantine edifice with white domes atop spiral pillars on the roof. I'd seen nothing like it before.

I stole ten minutes to wander around the cathedral on my own, taking photos of the dramatic frescos within. I found it slightly creepy that such an imposing religious building could sprout from such a poor, rural area. I guess that the extra-wide gap between rich and poor is nothing new in Romania.

It turns out that Manole – the previous night's rejected hotel – was actually the name of the Cathedral's architect. Legend has it that he was employed by a Romanian prince to build the most beautiful church possible. While putting on the finishing touches with a tin of Ronseal Cathedral Roof Protector ('It does what is says on the parchment'), Manole and his workmen were supposedly asked by the prince if they could ever build a finer one. Manole nodded; which was the wrong answer.

The prince – who never wanted his church to be surpassed – then reputedly ordered the scaffolding to be torn down, leaving Manole and his workmen trapped on the roof. The gory ending is that the builders all attempted to construct wooden wings so they could fly back to the ground, but each failed and fell to their deaths. Maybe they should have been less ambitious and used the wood to build a large ladder instead?

Still, at least Manole's spirit survived long enough in his broken body to request that his name live on, preferably as a sign above the door of a hotel that seemed a bit like a prison.

And so it came to pass.

From Curtea de Arges it would have been easy enough to follow the same road south towards the capital Bucharest, and onwards to our final destination. But that would be too simple. Instead we headed east towards Campulung and then on to Castle Bran; adopted home of the Dracula legend.

No sooner had we left Curtea than we also left the 21st century. Our scooters became time machines on a course set for the past. Were it not for the rubber tyres on the horse-drawn carts and the TV aerials on the tiny cottages, then we could have gone back 150 years. In this ancient rural community hay is not baled into brick-shaped slabs or drums wrapped in black plastic – it's stacked on wooden frames in conical haycocks. As we rode in the sunshine everything around was based on agriculture. We took cheery waves from bee-keepers and young lads delivering wood by horse and cart.

'This', said Tracy over the intercom system, 'is the real Romania'

I suspected that the scenery and the pace of life reminded her of childhood family holidays to Ireland's west coast where her uncles still worked the land. Maybe Romania was growing on her at last.

Sadly, like Ireland before its recent boom and bust, the real Romania has roads that are totally and utterly fucked. It has always amused me that every major road building project in Britain up to the mid-'90s seemed to be run with gangs of Irish navvies, but if you ever went to Ireland the roads were so shocking that it was hardly a good advert for their competence.

Well, you can say what you like about the roads in Ireland but I've never experienced such a shoddy, appallingly patched, bomb-site of a road as the 73C. I spent the next 42km at little more than 30mph swerving over both sides of the roads simply to pick the smoothest path through the craters. Tracy meanwhile was audibly losing enthusiasm for the 'real Romania', with every spine-jarring crash of her front wheel, as the forks bottomed out in yet another unavoidable pit.

At our lunch stop I surveyed the damage to the Maicoletta. A mist of oil from leaking oil-seals caused trails of dirt to stick to the fork legs. We could live with that; even before we left the seals weren't a perfect fit on the worn 1950s fork legs. What we couldn't live with was that the bumpy road had blown the gaskets out of the bolt-on fork bottoms. Fork oil was now gathering on the bolt heads and dripping onto the tarmac at an alarming rate.

There was very little damping in these primitive forks to begin with, but this problem would see the end of what little remained. If the fork legs were left to run totally dry then pretty soon the metal-on-metal sliding action would trash every component. The 'real Romania' was rapidly killing the Maico's forks.

I didn't want to think about trying to replace the forks if they suffered any further damage. Unmodified original ones are extremely rare, but these forks, adapted with a specially machined and welded bracket to suit the disc brake, were unique in the world. Perhaps bringing heavily modified scooters to such remote places wasn't such a clever idea after all.

Thankfully the road improved slightly as we headed for the handsome town of Campulung; which unfortunately sounds like a respiratory condition you can catch from sleeping in mouldy tents. Right in the centre of the town my clutch cable snapped and the city's stunning tree-lined boulevard was turned into a makeshift pit area.

The routine for clutch cable repair on a Lambretta is hard-wired into any rally going scooterist. Step one is tools out. Hunt for new clutch inner cable in spares bag. Discover clutch cable is the only one you've forgotten to bring. Beg clutch cable from better prepared riding companion. Lubricate cable with 2-stroke oil. Remove clutch lever and remaining pieces of old cable. Pray that the outer cable will stay in position so that you can thread inner into position without taking the handlebars to pieces. Fail. Take headlight out and handlebar top off. Successfully thread new cable into position. Rebuild handlebars. Reattach cable and adjust. Put tools away and look for somewhere to wipe dirty hands.

The whole process took around 20 minutes during which time Sam and Kimberly found entertainment in taking photos and video of a medium-sized dog attempting to have sex with a really small dog in the middle of the road. Another medium-sized dog stood close-by throughout – either as a guard or possibly waiting its turn. When I say 'in the middle of the road' I mean to the extent that all the passing cars had to swerve around them. Even staff from the electronics store opposite came out to watch the copulating canines and laugh. No doubt Romania's stray dog problem was about to get a little worse.

Enough of this pornographic pooch pantomime; we had an appointment with an impaler of an altogether different nature: Vlad Tepes and the imposing Castle Bran.

The imposing Bran castle actually looked a bit pokey when we first saw it. It's the same one depicted on the cover of the book, but designer Lee has carefully enlarged it in Photoshop so you can actually spot it. In reality Bran castle is small, set on a low hill and surrounded by a veritable cornucopia of tat shops catering to a throng of tourists. Dean had been here more than a decade previously, and in that time Romania had really cottoned on to the concept of 'cash-in tourism'.

Sam and Kimberly made it abundantly clear after Lake Balaton that they would be happy in any hotel that had a pool, so we booked into nearby Hotel Wolf 2; which had the added bonus of an adventure playground. For the princely sum of 65 Euros a night we rented a triple room the size of Liechtenstein, overlooking Bran castle. As you may imagine, Hotel Wolf 2 was built in the grounds of Wolf 1, but what you might not expect would be Supermarket Wolf, which was the same size as a provincial Co-op, or Bowling Wolf attached to the Wolf Pizzeria. This reminded me of the dry comment in one Eastern Europe guide book which states that 'Romania has two sorts of food: Romanian food and pizza.'

While unloading the scooters outside Wolf 2, five high-spec BMW touring bikes arrived. Tracy acknowledged the riders as she took her bags off, but was totally ignored. This was the first deliberately rude encounter we'd had with motorcyclists on the entire trip.

That evening we elected for Romanian food in Restaurant Wolf; as an alternative to pizza. My fantastic main course was a round, hollowed-out crusty bread loaf with the top cut off and filled with delicious pork on the bone soup.

A few tables away were the ignorant BMW riders: a mixed nationality group who were awkwardly conversing in English as the easiest common language. The one who appeared to be struggling with it the most was a fat Australian biker, of the type that think t-shirts with large airbrushed murals of wolves stretched over beer bellies looks cool.

I guessed from snippets of conversation that the group consisted of a Romanian motorcycle guide and a mixed-bag of customers who'd flown in, and were riding hired bikes. I may have made one or two loud and snidey remarks about having ridden there and not just jumped on a plane, but still there was no reaction.

*Pork soup inside a loaf of bread, Bran.*

*Dukes of Hazzard style Dacia, Curtea de Arges.*

*Curtea De Arges Cathedral.*

*The real Romania. (Photo: Kim)*

*Pornographic pooch pantomime, Campulung. (Photo: Kim)*

# BRAN FLAKY
## Day 10: Bran (Romania) to Brasov

Dean and I arose early the following morning because we had a mission. We were going to head for the nearest big city – Brasov – on a quest for 2-stroke oil to replenish our depleted supplies, and for some gasket paper to repair the forks on the Maico. While getting ready to leave, one of the BMW riders came over. Sure enough he was the Romanian guide for the group; which consisted of Germans and the Australian, all of whom flew in and hired their bikes. He was actually a nice bloke who imparted some useful information, and he seemed impressed that we'd come so far on scooters.

Before setting off for Brasov I downloaded a city map to my Android tablet and looked up the address of the Google's highest-ranked parts supplier in the city. Navigation with the Nexus 7 tablet was not easy while it was held in the clear pouch of my tank bag, because the capacitive touch screen does not respond to a gloved finger.

Eventually, after 20 miles riding across a flat plain between the mountain ranges, we enter the city and work our way to the address given for 'Moto24.ro'. We spend 10 minutes on the correct piece of street looking for the door number of this mythical motorcycle shop. Eventually I ask in a downstairs restaurant and a waiter patiently leads me back up to the street and into a nearby courtyard where one of the doorbells is marked Moto24. Inside the door, in a room the size of a box bedroom, is a young woman sat at a computer with one small rack of motorcycle consumables behind her. If Moto24 is the biggest bike parts dealer in Brasov, where do they keep the smallest, in a matchbox?

I've grossly underestimated the size of the business. The girl opens another door and behind it is a second room the same size, with some more racking in it. Thankfully they do have just enough 2-stroke oil for both of us, but not all of one brand. It turns out that Alex, who comes to assist us and speaks perfect English, only started Moto24 as a spin-off from his main travel agency business. Looking at his smart and professional website you'd never guess that it was a mail-order operation run from the corner of a travel agency.

Alex has worked really hard to get his shop to the top of the search rankings and is extremely pleased to know that we discovered it using Google. However we are not the first to expect more behind such an impressive web site. That is why his next venture will be to open a bricks and mortar shop, catering mainly to the Motocross market.

This is one of the problems with the internet. Everything is not what it seems. There are mail order businesses with professional-looking web sites that turn out to be one bloke in his bedroom, with zero stock, who simply takes a cut to arrange 'drop-shipping' from a wholesaler's warehouse. Equally there are 'internet scooterists' who are quick at giving opinions on scooter forums but you don't ever see riding a scooter. As Dean says; 'Some of them do thousands of miles on Facebook...'

Alex is really helpful though. Having bought his entire stock of Putoline 2-stroke oil, he gives us directions to a place where we might be able to buy some of the special paper needed to make new gaskets for the Maico forks. Sadly Moto24's stock did not include any sufficiently thick fork oil, but we aren't disheartened. Oil is basically oil and we could always use Automatic Transmission Fluid or even 2-stroke oil as a last resort. In such basic forks, anything is better than nothing.

Next stop is the bearing shop that Alex directed us to. Inside the lady behind the counter looks as sour as a mouthful of lemons. With difficulty we manage to explain our requirement for a small 10cm x 10cm piece of gasket paper. She in turn explains that we could only have the whole sheet of 1-metre by 1.5 metres, at a cost of around £25. We explain that we didn't really need that much, and the conversation quickly grinds down into a Small Faces stalemate of 'all or nothing'.

Thankfully I notice that they also sell motorcycle fork oil in our required grade. No sooner have I bought a bottle than the owner appears, and everyone becomes more helpful. Suddenly I am no longer a timewaster, and yes, I can have just a small strip of gasket paper.

I suppose our initial demand seemed a little like going in to a corner shop and asking for two slices of bread to make a sandwich, if only the shop-keeper would be so kind as to open a whole loaf.

Once back at Wolf 2 we dragged the Maico under some shade and proceeded to rebuild the forks. Dean went into Boy Scout mode and whittled me a new pair of perfect-fitting gaskets with a pen-knife. Meanwhile I set up an intravenous drip with a large syringe and some thin hose in order to fill the Maico's forks back up with the right amount of oil.

For a test ride on the repaired Maico, Dean and I took the kids to visit Bran Castle; which required Sam to miss an appointment with death-slide Wolf.

To say that Bran castle left me unimpressed is to make it sound better than it actually was. It is without doubt the worst exit-through-the-gift-shop tourist trap I have ever wasted time and money on.

Dean made it clear that it could be worse, as indeed it was when he first visited in 1996. At that time, the contents of the castle consisted of badly stuffed bears surrounded by dummies dressed in 1970's Romanian scarecrow attire. Back then the only mention of Dracula was in lop-sided lettering on woolly jumpers being knitted by fat gypsy women in the car park below the castle.

The castle itself is quaint enough but we had to pay to park the scooters, before ascending into what is actually a fortified house full of odd bits of historic furniture and innumerable information panels about the history of the Romanian royal family. Dean entertained us by slyly removing some of the velvet ropes that separated tourists from places they weren't supposed to visit, and watching as they got lost or told off by castle employees.

What Castle Bran was really short of, was anything relating to the only person tourists are really interested in – Vlad 'the impaler' Tepes – the bloodthirsty Wallachian king who inspired the Dracula novel. Maybe all the juicy info was in the 'torture' room; which you had to buy an additional ticket to access. Having been mugged once to enter the castle, we weren't going to compound our disappointment by paying again. 'Once bitten, twice shy', as they say in unsatisfying vampire-based tourist-trap support groups.

I'd done enough advance research to be aware that Bran's link with Vlad is actually pretty tenuous. He may once have stayed there, but it wasn't really his castle. Instead I get the impression that Bran has been associated with the Vlad Dracul legend chiefly because the castle is still complete, and there is ample parking space for coaches nearby.

If I'd done a bit more research I would have found out that Vlad's real castle – Poenari – was actually just off the Transfagarasan, and we'd effectively ridden straight past it. Having said that, it turns out that not much remains of Poenari apart from some earthquake damaged ruins, and these have actually been partly 'restored' by more Laurel and Hardy workmen using red house-bricks.

What is not in dispute is that Vlad was one bad dude. Legend has it that he impaled 20,000 people on a forest of wooden spikes near his capital of Targoviste. When it came to attacking the Ottomans south of the Danube it seems that Vlad was not fussy who he killed. Men, women and children were all fair game. Reputedly he delighted in perverse cruelty, such as slicing off the breasts of female prisoners and forcing their husbands to eat them, before putting them all on spikes anyway. Perhaps even more perversely, Vlad's victories were celebrated by the Vatican as a Christian king defending lands against the Muslim Ottomans.

I doubt that the holy books of either 'religion of peace' advocate turning people into shish kebabs. That's the trouble with things that are left open to interpretation: people only tend to follow the bits that suit their personal agenda. You'd think that 'thou shalt not kill' was a fairly straightforward instruction though…

Romanians seem able to overlook Vlad's excesses, and some still regard him as a national hero. Certainly there are plenty of streets named after Vlad Tepes dotted around the country.

*Dean carves a new fork gasket from a hard-won sheet of gasket paper.*

*Stripping the Maico forks to fit new gaskets, Bran. (Photo: Tracy)*

*An intravenous drip set up to refill the Maico's fork oil.*
*(Photo: Tracy)*

# COMMUNIST CULTURE CRIMES
## Day 12: Bran (Romania) to Bucharest

High in the sky, the clouds that we'd evaded at Lake Balaton were plotting their revenge, as we readied ourselves for departure from Wolf 2. Donning cheap plastic waterproofs in such heat and humidity is a pointless task, because everything you wear close to the skin soon becomes sweatier than a boxer's butt crack. As such, I urged everyone to get ready quickly against a sound-track of thunder echoing around the surrounding mountains.

The rushing proved worthwhile; only a few spits of moisture hit us before, once again, we outran the coming storm. Our route headed southeast across a wide, winding mountain pass before meeting the A1 road that runs due south to Bucharest.

This was a public holiday in Romania; which has all the same connotations as in England. With the chance of a long weekend off work, everyone from the city was fleeing either to the Black Sea coast or north to the mountains. Every tourist trap town on our route was a bustling hubbub, with a long jam on the opposite side of the road leading to each one. As a former London resident I have little patience for traffic jams, but it seemed that the single lane road north of Ploiesti offered no alternatives to drivers but to suffer in silence.

How wrong I was. The driver of the 4x4 car moving head-on for us had clearly decided to improvise his own chaotic escape route. With two wheels in our lane and two wheels scrabbling for grip in the roadside dirt, he sent the vehicles in front of us swerving around while he ploughed relentlessly towards oncoming traffic. Maybe it was some kind of emergency like his wife was giving birth? More likely his ice creams were melting.

From Ploiesti south we were now on a featureless plain, so Dean's accidental navigation onto the motorway for Bucharest was a blessing. Oddly, the motorway was sparsely occupied, save for a few Bucharest elite in fast cars and a Porsche police car employed to spoil their fun. For once the freshly laid tarmac was smooth and allowed steady progress through a land dotted with oil wells and the kind of hammer-headed pumps that you normally associate with Texas or Kuwait.

This oilfield was the main source of fuel to the Nazi war machine during WWII. As such it was targeted in 1943 by the Americans in a daylight bombing raid called Operation Tidal Wave. The mission was one of the costliest air operations of the war, resulting in the loss of 660 men and 53 USAF aircraft. It was also a tragic waste of effort. Within only a few weeks the repaired Ploiesti oilfields were producing more fuel than before the bombing.

Gradually Bucharest hove into view, and the view was not pretty. The outskirts of capital cities very rarely are. This northern section of the hive is where the drones live.

Entering the capital on a bank holiday meant that traffic chaos and manic drivers were mostly absent. I navigated with Sam holding the tablet over my lap, but this proved challenging and confusing because every pothole and tram track made the screen orientation switch round, so north briefly became south, or east. Remembering to turn off the auto-rotate feature would have helped.

Despite these challenges we found our centrally-located hotel – the Michelangelo – without much trouble. The hotel staff wanted a token fee to bring the scooters into their long courtyard, but it was a small price to pay for secure parking in a city centre.

Bucharest – when we went exploring by foot – appeared to be set out as islands of beauty surrounded by oceans of ugly. Despite the fact that we were in one of the better neighbourhoods of the old town, litter remained a constant feature. My cousin Michael – who lives in Bucharest – describes Romania as a 'cross between Switzerland and Stoke'. I had a strong suspicion that we'd left the Switzerland part of the country behind us and landed very firmly in the Stoke section.

One of the things that became immediately clear was that Ceausescu – who became devoutly atheist after his conversion to born-again communism – was not prepared for anything to stand in the way of his totalitarian vision. He destroyed 20 churches and thousands of homes to redevelop the centre of the city, but an odd few places of worship remain. The rather handsome brick church on Boulevard Nicolae Balcescu was built between the wars by the Italian government. Diplomatically, Ceausescu decided not to bulldoze it. Instead it has been aesthetically insulted, surrounded on three sides by taller, squarer buildings that gather around it like a gang of muggers. Another eight historic churches were laboriously dismantled, moved to other locations and rebuilt to satisfy the dubious communist grand plan.

Now it looks very much like there is no plan at all. Certainly whoever carried out electrical wiring in the old city is not working to any standards that would be acceptable to the west of Hungary. Massive telegraph poles carry knotted loops of cables that look like something a monkey might produce if you gave him an old cassette tape to play with.

This same street carries memorials to those who died in 1989 during the first headlong push to freedom from dictatorship. The removal of Ceausescu solved only one problem for Romania, but many remain: poverty, litter, ageing population and packs of stray dogs, to name a few. Tackling these must be as frustrating as trying to pack your shadow into a box. Presumably that's why many instead prefer to emigrate. The Daily Mail would have you believe that the 12% population reduction (2.6 million people) in the decade up to 2012 would mostly be gipsies coming to Britain to claim benefits and sell the Big Issue. In reality much of the exodus consists of younger, better educated Romanians who are simply looking to improve their standard of living. In their position I'd probably do the same thing…

That evening is an interesting one. Dean gets in touch with a Romanian contact called Andrei Bucur who owns one of very few

Lambrettas in Romania. Sadly it isn't running, but he still takes the time to drive 40km into Bucharest with his brother to meet us. Andrei purchased the TV175 from a staff member of the Italian Embassy who brought it over in the 1960s. This sleek, capitalist machine must have caused quite a stir amongst the residents of Bucharest when it was ridden around the city. While Innocenti did briefly list a Lambretta importer for Romania in their literature, classic vehicle enthusiast Andrei does not know of any other surviving examples.

My cousin Michael also comes to visit us with his Romanian wife Aurore and their two-year-old son Max. Michael works as editor/reporter on an investigative journalism website called www.theblacksea.eu.

Mike had recently completed work on a documentary film called 'Man's Best Friend' about an issue we'd already experienced: namely Romania's stray dog problem. At the time of writing there were thought to be around two million stray dogs in the country. There were also several instances where people had been killed by packs of dogs, which prompted a national debate about the problem and potential solutions.

A month after our trip the government voted in favour of a 'euthanasia' programme for dogs captured from the street, and not claimed by anyone within 14 days. This is an unconventional use of the term 'euthanasia'; which is a word normally associated with terminally ill people who have chosen to die. A more accurate phrase would be a 'cull' or 'extermination programme' because I guess that few of these healthy but unwanted dogs were contemplating suicide.

One interesting conversation concerns our next destination – Bulgaria – and the Romanian attitude towards it. I find it odd that neither Aurore nor Michael – who are both pretty worldly wise – have ever visited Bulgaria when the border is less than 50 miles away. Andrei had been through it by car on his way to Turkey, but was not very positive about the experience.

The irony of the Hungarians warning us about the Romanians before we crossed the border, only for the Romanians now to warn us about the Bulgarians has not escaped me. It is a fact of human nature that much of the prejudice that exists in the world is reserved for your nearest neighbours. That might mean the ones in your street or the next nearest country. For the English it's usually jokes about the Irish or 'cultural difficulties' with the French.

During our discussions in Bucharest we are told that the Bulgarian police operate random road blocks solely with the intention of handing out fines to foreigners. Andrei suggests we keep a few 5-Euro notes to hand in case we are stopped by coppers looking for a bribe. Apparently Romanians are considered well-off in Bulgaria and therefore ripe for exploitation.

We hear cultural stereotypes about the Bulgarians having 'fat necks', and that they are terrible drivers. We are even told that the roads are worse than Romania, though I personally doubt that this can possibly be true, unless the entire country is one enormous ploughed field.

Bulgaria does not get a good review, but this has no effect on our plans. Like Hungary we have no preconceptions about the country, other than the fact that we've got to cross it to get to Istanbul.

*Mike and Max, Bucharest. Note the reserve*
*rear hub inside Dean's spare wheel.*

*The aesthetically bullied Italian church, Bucharest.*

*Romanian Lambretta owner Andrei Bucur (left)*
*and his brother Dan, Bucharest.*

# DANUBE DETOUR
## Day 13: Bucharest (Romania)
## To Pomorie (Bulgaria)

I make the mistake of relying on my directionally-retarded Sat Nav to steer us out of Bucharest, despite the fact that the screen only shows main roads. My Garmin is a Western Europe model, so it can hardly be blamed for this lack of detail. Typically, this means that we are directed to a motorway, which is not ideal, but this motorway doesn't even seem to be going the right way.

Dean is content to let me navigate for the most part, not only because I've got the navigation equipment, but also a reasonably reliable internal compass. He does keep an eye on the position of the sun though, to ensure we are heading in roughly the correct direction. As a team, we're very much an unholy mating of digital and analogue.

At this point we are casting shadows to our left side, making it obvious that we are heading eastwards. The road we wanted for the Bulgarian border was almost due south from Bucharest. Something is definitely wrong.

I'm already aware of the mistake when we pull over in a lay-by to check the map on my tablet. The news isn't good. It is 25 miles back to Bucharest and there are very few junctions off the motorway where we could turn back. Instead I propose that we keep heading east along the north bank of the Danube and find another border crossing further along the river.

We agree to get off at the next motorway junction in order to look for fuel and check the maps in more detail. There is no choice but to carry on for mile after mile of dull dual carriageway, on which Dean's overburdened GP struggles to exceed 50mph whenever it hits a hill or a headwind. True to form, he waves both of us past so he can suffer alone, while we keep up a comfortable 65mph whatever the conditions.

This motorway has a decent surface, like the one we used into Bucharest, but it is nowhere near as quiet. Tracy and I occasionally need to overtake a slow lorry, but entering the fast lane is a real lottery due to the aggressive driving style of the richer Romanians. They are still heading for the coast in fast German saloon cars, presumably desperate to catch up with the bank holiday vibe. We don't see any police cars to prevent this behaviour, but we do pass several civilian highway agency vehicles. We have a similar service in Britain to clear crashes, breakdowns and hold-ups.

While our Frankenstein scooters may need maintenance to exposed drive chains and one-off components, they were specifically modified to cope with motorway speeds and have enough acceleration to blast around a slow-moving vehicle in a matter of seconds. By contrast Dean's under-powered Lambretta may be reliable but it's not very fast. On this motorway he chose to ride in the hard shoulder on the long uphill sections, simply to avoid causing an obstruction. He has effectively brought a spoon to a steak dinner: he'll get there in the end but it'll be hard work.

At the next junction we pull off as agreed to wait for Dean to catch up, only to find a police car waiting in the lay-by.

As soon as Dean arrives the young Romanian policeman approaches and, in very good English, asks to see the documents for Dean's scooter. It's immediately apparent what is going on. One of the highway agency cars has spotted Dean's snail-like progress on the motorway and reported it to the police. In Romania – as in Britain – there is a minimum engine capacity of 50cc for motorway use, and the policeman suspects that Dean is riding some sort of moped. Dean then points to the '200' badge on the legshields which momentarily puts the copper off the scent.

It is clear that our new friend is enjoying showing off his English, so before any further progress is made towards looking over the scooter or its documents, I ask for help with directions. I explain that we are heading for Turkey and are a little off track in our attempt to cross into Bulgaria. PC Plod explains that we should go back 40 miles to Bucharest and then head south, but I enquire if it is possible to continue following the motorway east and find another crossing into Bulgaria further on. Our new friend suddenly loses all interest in Dean's Lambretta and instead becomes an oracle of useful information. Not only does he offer a route, but also the position of every service station on the motorway.

The policeman explains that our next potential border is to cross the Danube from Calarasi in Romania to Silistra in Bulgaria. The quickest way to Calarasi is to return to the junction and rejoin the motorway. Of course Dean's scooter is still no faster on the highway than it was five minutes before, but all that matters in the eyes of the law is that it meets the minimum engine requirement; which it does.

All across central Europe from its source in Germany, the 2,872km long Danube serves as a natural dividing line between countries. Here it marks Romania's southern border with Bulgaria, before the river diverts north towards Ukraine.

We catch our first sight of the mighty Danube after passing through Calarasi. To be fair it is much smaller and narrower than I imagined. I'm sure many women have experienced similar disappointment at times; though obviously not with me.

Since we had never planned to use this route, we had no idea whether to expect a bridge, a tunnel or a ferry to get across the river. In the end it was none of them.

We rode into a Calarasi's grand 10 Million Euro ferry terminal (built in 2007 mainly with EU grant money) only to find it closed for business. Apparently the Romanian and Bulgarian companies set up to run the service had fallen out, and for a long while the route was suspended.

Now, thankfully, there was an operational service of sorts, but to call it a ferry is like saying that a birthday balloon is an aircraft. Our international freight transport device consisted of a large metal raft tied to a tugboat with bits of wire. The flat, rusting steel deck had strips of thick rod welded to it for tyre adhesion. The platform offered a total capacity of a lorry or two and some cars; basically as much as they could cram on without it sinking.

I knew instinctively that Tracy would be worried about getting the heavily loaded Maicitbetta on and off the stepped ramp onto the barge. We had no spare levers with us, nor do I have a spare wife, so there really was very little room for error. After buying tickets in a booth at the side of the jetty we were the last to be loaded behind several Ukrainian cars driven by men the size of bears. I rode the Maicoletta on board before returning to collect my scooter from the jetty.

Out of habit I tried my best to memorise which of the many decks the scooters were on, before heading to the bar. It doesn't pay to get lost. In reality the only deck is zero and the only bar is whatever drinks were strapped to our luggage. Mid-way across the Danube, which was not blue but more of a dirty grey-green, our battered tug – Cardinal – passed its sister boat – Perla – taking a similar load back across the river. I peered ashore to find the road for unloading on the Bulgarian side, but it appeared that nobody had bothered to build one. The only thing to greet us was a metal jetty and a gravel dustbowl leading off through the trees. My heart sank. Maybe the Romanians were right about the state of Bulgarian roads.

As soon as a few vans unloaded I had space to move and rode the Maicoletta from the raft while Tracy walked off with the kids. Then I had a sprint back to the barge to collect my Lambretta. Now if only I could remember which deck I'd parked it on. Ah yes – deck zero.

The lack of tarmac and the sudden inability to read anything due to the use of Cyrillic characters made our entry to Bulgaria both harsh and intimidating. Once we eventually found Bulgarian passport control, we were asked for our documents by a severe looking immigration officer. He had the same talent for English that Professor Stephen Hawking has for the 400-metre hurdles. After scanning the documents for each scooter, simply to check that the names on the passports matched those on the log books, he let us go. In the new Europe of the Schengen Treaty we are supposed to be able to move freely through member countries without this sort of nonsense. At least it gave us a little warm-up for the Turkish border experience yet to come.

International port towns – as a fairly reliable rule of thumb – are horrible places, and you should get out of them as soon as you can. Silistra proved no exception, but the mood on the intercom began to lift a little, as soon as we realised Bulgaria was not made up of bumpy cart tracks, and actually had better road surfaces than Romania.

Exiting the town, we passed a massive row of sculptures all made from rubbish. Collections of clear plastic drinks bottles were transformed into pirate ships, aeroplanes or animals; which I feel is a far better use for them than simply littering the countryside.

Almost immediately, rolling hills replaced the plains and mountains of Romania. The inclines meant that Dean's progress was slow so he waved us ahead again. Northern Bulgaria seemed strangely reminiscent of the hilly farmlands of West Country Britain, except that the crops were mostly sunflowers rather than wheat or rape-seed. We passed an airfield where every aeroplane had a propeller and two sets of wings. This nation is certainly retro.

Throughout the trip I made a point of waving to people at the roadside to check out their reaction. Typically the closer you get to a city the less likely you are to get a response, because city dwellers tend to be cynical and suspicious. Here though, in rural Bulgaria, almost everyone waved back; which was an encouraging sign. Even the faster cars that we waved past flashed their indicators to say thank you afterwards. These were not the hot-head drivers that we had been warned about either.

After half an hour's riding we stopped to wait for Dean at a lay-by where about ten different stallholders were selling fruit. I pulled to the far end so as not to disturb their trade, only for one of the ladies to come across to us after a few minutes with a bag of three peaches. She made it clear that these were a gift and with profuse thanks she simply walked back to her stall. The peaches were, quite simply, the most delicious I've ever tasted: flavoursome without being ridiculously juicy. What is more, they represented a genuinely friendly welcome to a new country.

Tracy and Sam went back to try and pay for the peaches despite the fact that we only had Romanian Lei, only for the lady to give us another six peaches for free. By the time Dean arrived – having stopped for fuel and paid by card – we had collectively decided that we liked Bulgaria, and Tracy already preferred it to Romania.

Our route took us via the town of Dobrich, where we were in dire need of both Bulgarian money and something quick to eat.

Parked outside a café on the way into town was the most outlandish iron-curtain motorcycle and sidecar, flying a red flag. The two outfit pilots quickly donned leather tank commander helmets and gave chase, before briefly giving us an escort into the centre. Despite the poor, rural nature of the countryside, the town was modern and bustling.

Obtaining cash from a hole in the wall was as easy as ever, but anything written in Bulgarian presented more of a challenge. With time now tight due to our Romanian detour, Dean and I elected to pick up takeaway kebabs on the pedestrianised high-street. Unable to read the kebab shop's menu I resorted to pointing at the chicken and chip wraps bought by the previous customer. Any worries over the ordering process soon evaporated once the lady serving explained, in perfect English, that she'd spent eight years working in Portrush, Northern Ireland. Cue that shrinky-world feeling.

After Dobrich we headed south towards the coast; which we met at the port town of Varna. From there we followed the sea, on a route of beautiful twisting roads through endless Black Sea coastal colonies. Road signs proclaimed that apartments in these new developments could be purchased for as little as £18,000. While the prices may be keen, the resorts looked very much like they had been thrown up in obscure places without good access to the sea, and with little local infrastructure to support them.

One thing the Romanians were right about, though, was the presence of police checks along the road. At various points large groups of armed coppers carried out vehicle stop and search, but our scooters didn't even register on their radar. Those being stopped were usually big blokes in big cars with the boot of each vehicle being thoroughly investigated.

In a petrol station approaching the resort of Sunny Beach we came across a mob, literally, of the very latest high-end Audis and Porsches, each packed with body-builder types in their mid-30s. One of the minders, standing in front of me in shorts, had the most beautiful tattoo work on his tree-like legs. The images included a depiction of a historic Bulgarian soldier in dress uniform on his calf. I thought it wise to ask if I could take photos of the artwork, only to be given an internationally clear shake of the index finger, which was handy because Bulgarians nod for 'no' and shake their heads for 'yes'.

I'm sure that secretly the meathead was proud of his tattoo, but obviously it would be a breach of gangster etiquette to start showing ink to interested tourists. Instead they did their best to maintain a cool air of menace while I made similar efforts to ignore their unsubtle parading. Let's be straight, the only people that age with such expensive cars are wealthy footballers, chart-topping musicians or criminals. From the look of these guys you'd guess that the only balls they'd been kicking lately still had the owner attached.

Thankfully our hotel booking was past the Mafiosi haunt of Sunny Beach, and on to the family-friendly resort of Pomorie. You couldn't get more welcoming than our hosts Petar and Margarita at Viva Beach Hotel. After making it clear that we were unhappy about parking our scooters on the seafront strip overnight, they allowed us to move some of their restaurant tables and put the bikes in the courtyard until breakfast. That evening Dean and I discussed our encounter in the petrol station with a local Bulgarian lad. He explained that certain families who owned coastal land had become rich very quickly through development deals. With the money came a certain attitude, and as a result of their ostentatious lifestyle these high rollers had to travel everywhere with minders. In small ponds like this there are always a bigger fish to be wary of.

'They are stupid people who do not know how to live', he said. 'I do not think that they sleep well at night.'

We had no such problems. After our first paddle in the Black Sea, we slept fantastically.

*Transport across the Danube.*

*The road into Bulgaria after the Danube river crossing. (Photo: Kim)*

*Tracy and Sam being given free peaches, Bulgaria.*

*Our escort into Dobrich. (Photo: Kim)*

*Police checks, Bulgaria. (Photo: Sam)*

# TALKING TURKEY
## Day 14: Pomorie (Bulgaria) to Vize (Turkey)

Petar and Margarita were the perfect hosts, so it pained us to leave Bulgaria after only a single night. If their son – who is studying hotel management in London – has learned any skills from his folks, then he's got a bright future even without the degree.

Despite only staying a single night, the couple presented us with a bottle of wine as a memento when we left. Dean doesn't drink wine, so sadly Tracy and I were forced to commandeer that bottle for later, hopefully to celebrate our arrival in Istanbul.

Ironically, if the Islamist Turkish prime minister had his way, we would not be able to drink it there at all. Alcohol culture is something that Recep Tayyip Erdogan is restricting, and would prefer to ban entirely, along with kissing in public.

Two months prior to our departure Turkey had been rocked by protests and riots which had their epicentre in Istanbul. Initially sparked by a government plan to redevelop Gezi Park by building a mosque and a shopping centre, this rapidly became a nationwide uprising by secular and liberal Turks against Erdogan's increasingly dictatorial government. Erdogan countered these demonstrations not only with force on the streets, but by arresting journalists, union leaders, and anyone capable of stoking the fires of unrest.

News of the protests subsided before we left, but that didn't necessarily mean things were stable enough for us to travel there without issue. Newscasters know that their audiences are fickle and will quickly switch spotlight to another subject if they sense that the public's bombarded attention span is drifting.

Would Istanbul be safe when we arrived?

Who knew?

Before we could worry about Turkey we had to get into it. The route from Burgas to the border crossing at Malko Tarnovo turned out to be a fantastic biking road; one of the best of the whole trip. A fresh, smooth sinew of tarmac wound its way though tree-lined mountain roads. Dean and Kim spotted a dead, bloated horse at the side of the road, but Tracy and I were well ahead and too busy enjoying the freshly laid surface to notice even large deceased mammals. Then, three kilometres from the border, the road suddenly deteriorated into the sort of bumpy, broken mess that the Romanians would be proud of.

When we arrived at the Bulgarian border there was a long queue of around 30 cars at a standstill. Dean, as politely as ever, got off and waited in true English style.

I have a slightly different, some might say hypocritical, outlook on the matter as it relates to riding a two-wheeler. Others might call it pragmatic.

One of the main reasons I ride a scooter is that I have no intention of sitting in queues at junctions or traffic lights, when I can ride straight to the front. In the UK this practice is called 'filtering' and it is perfectly legal, as it is in many civilised countries. In others, like Germany, filtering to the front of the traffic is forbidden. Bikers are supposed to sit behind the cars and wait, even if it is snowing and your cold fingers must be prised from the handlebars with a crow-bar at the end of your journey.

Bollocks to that.

I tend to look at it this way. If each set of traffic lights takes two minutes to go from stop and back to green, then every time I sit in a queue and miss a sequence of lights, it wastes two minutes of my life. I'm never going to get that time back and there are better things I could do with two spare minutes rather than sitting impotently in a queue like a car driver. Hell, that's enough time for foreplay. Twice.

When it comes to foreign travel, rather than going through all the unnecessary rigmarole of checking the filtering legislation in each country, which might be tricky even with Google, I find the best solution is just to do what the locals do. Then, if the locals still don't filter or 'make progress' as the British police call it, the best solution is to filter anyway and just pretend to be a stupid foreigner who doesn't know the rules. Actually, that's not true either. In reality you have to judge the situation and ask yourself this question:

*'If I push to the front here, am I going to obstruct anyone, and will I piss them off enough that they'll try to knock me off further down the road?'*

If the answer to both questions is an emphatic 'no', then go for it. Most car drivers in the city understand that having bikes filter to the front of a queue has absolutely no bearing on their overall journey time. The exceptions to this are if your scooter is slow to accelerate (like Dean's overloaded GP), or if you are going to cause a significant delay to those behind you. In other words; on occasions such as fumbling for passports at borders, or for change at toll booths.

Ignoring my own sage advice – a fairly consistent character flaw – I left the others queued behind the cars and rode to the front to find out what the delay was, and also to judge whether we'd be able to sneak up there on the scooters. One solitary motorcycle was parked at the front and its riders were smoking and talking with a group of people near the firmly closed border. The delay, they reported, was due to technical problems on the Turkish side. The Bulgarian guards expected that the Turks would have the border open by around 5p.m, which was still several hours away. I'm sure that if you were heading in the opposite direction then the Turks would be blaming the Bulgarians for the delay. The reality was probably that both sides closed their border offices for lunch.

Before I had time to return with the awful news, there was a sudden flurry of activity. Drivers stubbed out fags and ran back to their vehicles as the Bulgarian official raised his barrier. Turkey – it seemed – was now open for business.

Around the corner was another stop, still in Bulgaria, and Dean dutifully joined a queue of cars being dealt with extremely slowly. Impatiently I rode to the front, only to find that this line was for a document that wasn't even applicable to bikes. Patience and manners would have seen us all wasting half an hour in a queue that we didn't need to be in.

The way I look at it, in most cultures, bikes are always allowed to go first. If you go to the front and someone objects then just return to the back and you haven't lost anything. But if you don't try you'll never know.

The mildly infuriating process of leaving Bulgaria was a mere morsel compared to the bureaucratic banquet that awaited us on the Turkish side of the hill. We had been warned in advance that this border crossing would be a slow process, so we bought plenty of drinks and prepared ourselves mentally for a long haul.

The kids were left to guard the scooters while we joined an insane multi-national throng queuing inside the large single-storey border building. On each space of the wall was a different counter for one part of the rigmarole, but not a single sign or clue indicating in which order these processes should be tackled. Being British we decided the best course of action was just to join the end of the longest queue. That soon turned out to be an error, because this line was for people leaving Turkey.

The procedure was actually this:

- *Go to the visa desk, wait for the guy to return from the toilets, pay £10 (or 15 Euro) per person for a Turkish visa to be applied to your passport. Kimberly, who has an Italian passport, was not required to buy a visa.*
- *Join the passport control queue where they check that you have a visa. This counter is located next door to the man who just sold it to you.*
- *Wait in the vehicle documents queue. Or rather don't, because when you get to the front they'll send you away to get an insurance Green Card if you don't already have one. Look glumly at growing queue. If all goes well, the girl at the counter will encourage you to come straight back to the front with your Green Card.*

- *Buy insurance Green Card for your vehicle, because most EU insurance policies do not cover Turkey. We buy ours from a guy in a little booth outside the main building. He looks up 'Lambretta' on his computer system and cannot find such a vehicle. Dean digs us out of this stalemate by looking at the screen and telling the guy just to put the nearest thing (Vespa PX200) on the certificate along with each registration number. Clearly the rare Maicoletta must also become an honorary Vespa for the purposes of insurance. A Green Card for 30 days costs 45 Turkish Lire (roughly £15). Thankfully Tracy had the forethought to buy Turkish Lire in the UK because there were no cashpoints at the border. Without any local currency we would have been stuffed.*
- *Sheepishly return to the head of the now massive vehicle documents queue with all paperwork finally present and correct. Conduct pacifying mission with irate people at front to explain that you are not pushing in, and that the girl has asked you to return. At this point totally take the piss and ask her to sort the documentation for three bikes, not just the one you originally queued up for.*

It was interesting watching Dean, who as a youngster was trained in sales techniques and skills like use of body language, diffusing the situation with the angry people in the queue. I resisted the temptation to say 'Don't you know we are British my good fellow?' on the basis that any ironic attempt at Empire-based Raj humour would probably be taken at face value and we'd end up in a massive brawl.

My mate Alan made that very mistake in Ireland when we encountered a road-block as our club travelled en masse to a rally. We'd been told that the Garda were out checking Irish vehicles for road tax, so when Alan rode to the front of the queue and innocently explained 'It's ok I'm English', he didn't get a good reaction. In fact the apoplectic Irish policeman, was so angry I thought he was going to explode like a ginger Big Bang, fuelled by years of Irish (and ginger) repression.

After centuries of cack-handed, hypocritical military and diplomatic bungles by previous governments I think it's fair to say that holding a British passport is not a guarantee of first class treatment.

After we'd successfully sorted all our documents – which took around two hours in queues – we all remounted the scooters, only to be stopped again at Customs for another passport check.

Finally, free of the bureaucratic minefield, we pulled up to chat to three Turkish motorcyclists who were on their way back to Istanbul after a tour of Greece, Macedonia and Bulgaria. The trio were very friendly to the point of giving us their phone numbers if we needed any help in the city. They told us that to use the motorway network – which included both of the bridges over the Bosphorus River – you were supposed to have an HGS card. This road toll prepayment card includes a passive identity transmitter. HGS was introduced when cash tolls were abolished in 2012. The bikers explained that the motorway would be the best way for us to get into the city, but we'd already chosen to use the minor roads at the suggestion of Vespa rider Hassan, who we'd met in Hungary.

Our next plan was to pitch up near the fishing village of Kiyikoy on the Black Sea coast, and spend our first night under canvas with the kids. Let's just say that there was mixed enthusiasm for this within the group, but at the very least it would mean we hadn't carried camping gear 2,500 miles around Europe for nothing.

Turkey, after one final passport check to compound our border crossing misery, turned out to be an eye-opener. You don't need to cross the Bosphorus to feel like you are on another continent, it happens pretty much straight away.

To be fair the contrast between countries got more marked the further East we travelled. The European Union and global capitalism have ensured that Western Europe is a single homogenised corporate mess. Ride from Paris to Hamburg and you'll cross three borders without really noticing any change. The currency remains the same and the price for the McDonalds cardboard meal at the side of any motorway remains largely uniform. It's all as bland as the burger; which is what the architects of the EU seem to want. If they could wipe out national identity and have a giant single-language consumer super-state, then their dream would be realised, and my nightmare.

The whole point of travel is to see new and interesting things, so making everywhere the same defeats the purpose. Thankfully Eastern Europe retains some individual character. Aspirational Hungary still pulls closely towards Alpine Austria; despite the former's time behind the Iron curtain and their peculiar alphabet. Then there is an acute difference to Romania; whose language is sufficiently similar to Italian that Dean can understand much of it. After the cleanliness of Hungary, the litter and crumbling roads of Romania came as a real shock.

Over the border in Bulgaria the alphabet changes once more to something that would be utterly unreadable if it wasn't translated into Latin script on the road signs. From Romania to Bulgaria the people look physically different too; often stockier.

Crossing to Turkey, the lush green landscape of Bulgaria is swapped immediately for a dusty, scrubby vista more reminiscent of Greece. The towns are also markedly busier than sparsely populated Bulgaria.

We pass through the town of Pinarhisar in the middle of their market day and the traffic is absolutely insane. Vehicles and pedestrians come at you from every angle, on either side of the road. It's a bit like playing pinball when the multi-ball feature is activated. So many sights, sounds and potential hazards all compete for your attention. Dean is not impressed when I pull up in the middle of the craziness to see if he would like to use a cashpoint.

In Pinarhisar we are like beacons of alien behaviour, initially for the fact we are the only people riding two-wheelers while wearing crash helmets. These come in useful when Kim warns Dean over the intercom to pay attention to the teenager standing behind him while he is entering his PIN number. Despite this, I don't feel a threat from the people or the traffic.

As soon as you enter any busy metropolis you might as well forget any provincial notion of 'right of way' or the 'highway code'. The only law in these circumstances is the Indian concept of 'Might is Right' where each road user must naturally give way to anything bigger or heavier, but they may justifiably expect smaller and lighter things to get out of their way. Motorcycles are a long way down this particular pecking order, below lorries, busses and cars. However even a scooter can do serious damage to a pedestrian or cyclist, so it is their job to stay out of your way. This is a system that works, after a fashion, in some of the most heavily populated places on earth.

Our plan to camp by the Black Sea coast was abandoned in the face of a truly ferocious wind coming from exactly that direction. The gale would have made tent erection more like kite flying.

Tracy really struggled to control the heavily laden Maicoletta in the wind. One of the known problems of this machine is that it has solid wheels rather than spokes. In high winds there is little you can do to stop the scooter from changing lanes when the wheels are caught by a strong gust.

Our patience for riding in that blast soon waned, so we elected to stop at the first decent hotel. We found one in the ancient Thracian settlement of Vize, some 150km short of Istanbul. This part of the world has seen more rulers than a school lost property department.

The hotelier suggested a restaurant a short amble away near the centre of Vize. There we felt even more alien because not a single thing on the menu was in English and I understand just less than zero Turkish. Ordering was simply a question of going up to the counter and pointing at what we wanted. If the excellent kebabs (or kebap as they are usually written) were insufficient, then it was merely a matter of repeating the process until you were full.

One thing that happens on long trips is that you lose connection with the days of the week. Every day becomes a travelling day. In Vize though, it was Saturday and from a side street came the infectious beat of drumming, marking a wedding party taking place in a nearby square. If it was indoors then surely it would be rude to gatecrash, but when the party is in a public street between blocks of flats, then could it hurt to have a look?

One thing was for certain; nobody had scrimped on the entertainment. The stage carried a traditional band of haunting horn and string instruments backed by a powerful sound system and light show. In front of the stage the syncopating rhythms were directed by two standing drummers beating skins supported on shoulder harnesses. Some might find the horns jarring, but I was intoxicated by the piercing sounds and driving beats.

Say what you like about the Turks, they are certainly a patriotic bunch. Stood close by the stage was a slight, grey-haired guy in a white shirt with a red arm-band. His only role appeared to be holding aloft the Turkish flag throughout proceedings with a straight arm. Occasionally the strain would get to him and he'd swap from one hand to the other, but he held his stick with the tenacity of a terrier. Equally, many of the young men hogging the limelight in the centre of the dance-floor wore red shawls over their white shirts, with the Turkish flag embroidered in gold braid. Unusually, it seemed to be the young men who were quickest to the dance floor and least likely to leave.

What was absent, from a British perspective, were people drunkenly dancing to Abba and crying girls being sick in the toilets. These Turks don't know what they're missing.

*A free bottle of wine from Petar and Margarita, Pomorie, Bulgaria.*

*Communist war memorial, Bulgaria. (Photo: Sam)*

*Registering all the scooters as Vespas for Green Card purposes, Turkish border.*

*My Shoei helmet carrying both video camera and intercom.*

*Wedding party dancers, Vize.*

*Turkish wedding drummers.*

117

# THE MANIC METROPOLIS
## Day 15: Vize (Turkey) to Istanbul

'Holy shit Batman, what is that infernal racket?'

'That, Robin, is the Muslim dawn call to prayer, emanating from loudspeakers on the nearby mosque. You are going to have to get used to it here in Turkey.'

The poetic, echo-laden wailing that wakes us in our hotel room overlooking the street is an ear-piercing reminder that we've not only encountered another culture, but also a very different religion.

If I had to hold up score cards for impressive architecture then it's a close run thing between churches and mosques. I like the rocket-shaped minarets on the mosques because they look cool, but equally you can't help but be impressed by the stone-masonry, carvings and stained glass of a good cathedral. When it comes to the audio element of worship though, the Muslim faith has the job sewn up. Church bells rung on a Sunday simply do not have the same impact as the haunting and insistent Adhan being blasted into your ears several times a day. As a cultural experience it is fantastic. As something I had to live with constantly, I think it would get right on my tits.

Britain or Turkey, bells or Adhan, the effect on the populous seems pretty much the same as far as I can see. The vast majority of folk ignore the din and get on with whatever else it was that they were doing. In Britain most people save their interaction with religious institutions for births, deaths and marriages. I wondered if the same was true here.

On the way to Istanbul we stopped to do a nut & bolt check at a crossroads town called Subasi, while we waited for Dean. It turned out that three of Tracy's rear wheel nuts could be undone by hand, which again proved the value of this military routine. A few miles further and the wheel nuts would probably have been lost. Even further down the line the wheel would have become wobbly and maybe even fallen off. I can think of very few instances where that might be regarded as a good thing.

Here in rural Turkey there seemed to be a strange mix of eastern and western traditions. We saw a large gang of 'black leather jacket' bikers heading in the opposite direction. I even managed to get one or two to wave back; which would probably earn them a kicking for being so uncool as to acknowledge scooterists. Tracy noticed that one of the riders of these heavyweight bikes was a woman. That's a fairly liberated thing to see when you consider that stricter Islamic states like Saudi Arabia don't even permit women to drive. Conversely, when we stopped for a break at a roadside café the clientele were entirely male. While our mixed-sex group seemed to be breaking some unwritten rule, neither Tracy nor Kim felt any threat in these places for the way they were dressed. This part of Turkey seems fairly liberal and it would be a shame if that ever changed.

Gradually our circuitous route turned almost due south towards Istanbul. Steadily the single lane roads expanded into two or three carriageways, like tributaries meeting to form an estuary. Skyscrapers appeared over the horizon followed by the full insane magnificence of the metropolis stretching out in super-wide panorama.

Around 14 million people live in Istanbul – almost double the population of overcrowded London. We fell lucky to have entered the city on a Sunday, but even so the traffic soon intensified beyond all recognition. Life was not made any easier by the fact that we had to navigate by the sun, since my Sat Nav lady appeared to have few constructive opinions on our route. A quick glance at the map on the tablet suggested we'd taken a wrong turn, but it was easily corrected. I sensed that tensions were starting to run high, as they always do when people are hungry.

The solution was a small suburban kebab restaurant that had a row of delivery scooters lined up outside on a steep hill. The young manager, who spoke excellent English, recommended a 'mixed kebab', which turned out to be a massive platter covered in salad and large pieces of cooked meat. It looked like a scale model of a hillside where a whole herd of animals had been napalmed. The spiced meats tasted delicious but we were defeated by the portion size.

The map on my tablet showed us that even though we were well into the built-up part of the city, our destination in old town district of Fatih was still 20km away. The manager suggested that we back-tracked to join the motorway, but instead we elected to keep heading south until we found the Sea of Marmara. Once we met the water it would be impossible to go wrong, as long as we kept the sea on our right hand side.

It still took almost an hour to negotiate the insane traffic and find our accommodation at the Stone Hotel in Sultanahmet.

Each of us is perfectly capable of riding in heavy traffic but even we had to admit defeat when the only way for the Turkish motorcyclists to progress was to bump up the kerbs and ride along the pavement. I was still tempted to follow suit but asking Tracy and Dean to do the same on their heavily laden scooters would be totally unfair. Better to chill out and be patient, which I always find difficult.

Thankfully the hotel, which Lonely Planet rates as 'hands down, one of the best budget choices in the city', turned out to be exactly that, and more. While there were no secure parking places for bikes here in the tightly-packed cobbled streets of the old town, we found a prime spot opposite the hotel reception, covered by their CCTV. The young and enthusiastic hotel staff greeted us warmly, before providing a cool drink in the hotel garden. That seated area in the shaded yard was a glorious oasis of calm from the manic city.

Tracy, Sam and I benefited from a room upgrade to a most magnificent suite. The double bed was draped in lace curtains hung from the tall ceiling and a tiled Jacuzzi took pride of place in the centre of the room. Dean's chin hit the floor when he eventually saw it. I guess that this is the benefit of being the person who actually makes the booking.

Our slightly smug satisfaction was soon wiped away when Sam went back to the room to use the Jacuzzi, while Dean and I discussed plans in the walled enclave of the garden. Tracy persuaded Sam not to overfill the Jacuzzi, so that he wouldn't spill any water when he inevitably started to splash about, as excited 11-year old lads are prone to do. This precaution backfired, literally, when Sam pressed one of the many buttons which turned on a water jet. This jet should have been submerged had the bath been full, but instead it acted as a fountain, spraying a strong torrent of water all over the fancy double bed and turning one corner of the room into a paddling pool. Sam panicked and ran off, leaving Tracy frantically prodding various buttons in an attempt to avert a flood that would have seen Noah reach for his woodwork tools.

I was not impressed, but the hotel staff seemed to have encountered this sort of problem before. They were very good about supplying new towels and fresh bedding after we mopped up all the water.

Istanbul is every bit as fascinating and fantastic as I'd imagined, given its location at the crossroads of shipping moving north from the Mediterranean into the Black Sea, and on the old Silk Road route from Asia westwards into Europe.

This is a city that was founded by the Greeks as Byzantium before spending over a millennium as Constantinople. It was epicentre to the Byzantine Empire and the Greek Orthodox branch of Christianity. That is, apart from the years 1204-1261 after the city was sacked, burned and conquered by the knights of the 4th Crusade.

These mainly French and German knights were supposed to be heading to the Holy Land via Egypt, but instead attacked Constantinople as part of a Venetian-lead piracy mission. The treachery of this Latin endeavour against fellow Christians weakened the Byzantine cause. Their empire never fully recovered its previous might, leaving Constantinople a softer target when the Muslim

Ottomans conquered the city in 1453.

Under the Ottomans, religion and politics remained intertwined, until shortly after World War 1 when Mustafa Kemal Ataturk founded the secular Turkish state. This 90-year period of separation between government and religion has only recently been eroded under Prime Minister Erdogan's Islamist rule, but not everyone agrees with him.

Our first venture towards the shopping area of the Grand Bazaar showed that everything was not calm; despite a concerted effort to persuade tourists otherwise.

We stumbled upon an argument between a couple of middle-aged Turks which was steadily escalating from shouting and pushing, towards violence. The row had drawn both a crowd of onlookers, and a whole team of young policemen wearing navy blue t-shirts and baseball caps, all equipped with massive truncheons.

I took a few furtive photos of the argument, which the uniformed police seem incapable of calming down. On the periphery of the watching crowd I noticed several casually-dressed men stood with small walkie-talkies: more police in plain clothes. I get the impression that Prime Minister Erdogan – who was previously mayor of Istanbul – had the city pretty much on lock-down following the riots. The vocal protesting of two months earlier has been systematically crushed, seven people had died, and now the authorities seemed highly alert to any sign of trouble.

The argument moved off in the opposite direction. Before I could arrange to go back alone and photograph what was going on, it appeared to have erupted. Six massive police vans and shortly afterwards, one ambulance, headed for the disturbance.

Erdogan's response to the protests had been both brutal and thorough; painting the protesters as terrorists and arresting anyone that opposed him, from army generals to journalists. Istanbul didn't feel like a good place to be seen pointing a big camera in the wrong direction, so I made my way back to meet the others.

*Celebrating our arrival with a glass of Bulgarian wine at the Stone Hotel, Istanbul. (Photo: Sam)*

*A fight about to kick off in Istanbul.*

# ISTANBUL UNITED
## Day 16: Istanbul

The following morning I tried to talk to the young guys working in the hotel about the troubles, but they didn't seem keen. For those in the hotel trade, anything that puts off potential visitors must be a disaster. The lads preferred to talk about football: both of them being supporters of local club Galatasaray.

Despite not being a football fan I know the name of their team for two reasons. Firstly the brutal stabbing to death of Leeds fans Kevin Speight and Chris Loftus in 2000 by members of Galatasaray's notorious Night Watchmen hooligan firm. This made a lasting impact on me because Kev was also a scooterist who rode with Gemini and Leeds Central scooter clubs. Effectively, members of their tribe had murdered one of my tribe: not only another Englishman but also a fellow Scooterboy.

In June Galatasaray fans once more cropped up in the news: again not for anything to do with football. Quite uniquely supporters of the three main Istanbul football clubs – Besiktas, Fenerbahce and Galatasaray – put aside their feuds to save Istanbul's Gezi Park from redevelopment. They united in the mass protests against Erdogan's government, which many saw as a burgeoning fascist dictatorship. Supporters of major football clubs always hate their local rivals, so for the three factions to march together under the title 'Istanbul United' meant that they must really detest Erdogan.

The stars of this particular show were the Carsi – supporters of Besiktas – who not only succeeded in chasing off several armoured police vans with a commandeered digger, but also managed to hijack a police 'Toma' water cannon vehicle that was being used to aggressively break up the Gezi Park demonstrations.

There's a great transcript of a radio conversation between the police chief, who is instructing his vehicles to break down the barricades, and Toma 9 which is being driven by a Carsi hooligan called Vedat and is randomly spraying water.

'Toma 9!' radios the police chief, at his disobedient water cannon.

'I am Vedat, listening!' replies the cheeky hijacker.

'Oh, who is Vedat?'

'From the stadium, the drummer!'

'Toma 7, retreat!!' shouts the police chief to the other water cannons, as the penny finally drops.

On the face of it, even an unpopular, dictatorial government is better than what was happening to Turkey's southerly neighbour. A two-year civil war raged in Syria almost unabated and largely without foreign intervention, but all that was about to change. In two days time the world's media would be filled with photos of men, women and children killed by a poison gas release in a Damascus suburb.

Those of us located only one border crossing away, eating ice cream and ogling the architecture of the Blue Mosque and Ayasofya (previously Hagia Sofia cathedral) may as well have been light years away from these atrocities. Ironically, considering Constantinople's history of Latin Christians attacking Byzantine Christians, it seems that what is going on in Syria is much the same. This time the battle lines appeared to be drawn between different branches of Islam.

I spotted a sign in the Blue Mosque which explained that Muhammad wanted everyone to follow one god with one religion, but still Muslims ended up separating into different sects. These branches have spent subsequent centuries murdering each other right up to the present day; much as the different Christian sects have in places like Northern Ireland.

Ataturk – the founder of modern Turkey – is famously quoted as saying, 'I have no religion, and at times I wish all religions at the bottom of the sea.'

When you see the death and misery caused in the name of religion, it's difficult not to sympathise with that viewpoint.

*The view from the Stone Hotel roof over the Sea of Marmara.*

*The Blue Mosque, looking rather yellow.*

# RIDING INTO ASIA
## Day 17: Istanbul to Canakkale (Turkey)

As scooterists there remains one important job for Dean and I to do, while in Istanbul. It is symbolic for us both to ride our scooters across the River Bosphorus via one of bridges that link Europe and Asia. However this objective is not without its complications.

The daytime traffic gridlock in Istanbul makes Rome, Paris and London look like small provincial hamlets. I don't have any issue in riding through heavy traffic. As a former London scooter-courier I positively enjoy weaving through lines of cars when there's room to squeeze through and I know where I'm going. To me it's like a video game, except mistakes actually hurt and you only get one life. Istanbul though, is another league. My clutch hand was in a state of cramp entering the city on a relatively quiet Sunday, so I had no intention of tackling this ride during the working day.

Our solution to this conundrum was to make a 5a.m start, with Dean meeting me at the Lambrettas parked outside the hotel. Our plan was to cross the bridge in time for the sunrise and return before the traffic turned to treacle.

Even at that time of the morning, Istanbul is a surreal place. As I crept about in the gloom trying to remove my alarmed Xena disc lock without the siren going off, suddenly the morning silence was broken by the call to prayer echoing from loudspeakers on minarets all over the city. The 'Muezzin' who recite the call seem to stagger their lines from one mosque to its neighbour, so the song echoes and repeats from one ear to the other like a mad stereophonic experiment. This haunting sound resonates through both the city and the centuries.

Dean and I added to the din with the gurgle of warming two-stroke engines as we carved our way back down to the shore-line, through streets that are thousands of years and several civilisations old. My scooter suddenly felt alive again; free of both luggage and the responsibility of a pillion. As the night retreated under the sun's onslaught, I could finally misbehave again, letting my engine scream like a wounded banshee from the traffic lights.

Before leaving, I did my best to roughly memorise the route. Head over the Galata Bridge and up past Taksim – epicentre of the protests – before joining the motorway. There we jumped straight onto the Bogazici Bridge in order to cross the Bosphorus to the Asian side.

One vital ingredient for this trip was missing. Neither of us had the HGS prepayment card needed to access the motorway network. According to our Turkish friends the whole system was now entirely reliant on technology and number plate recognition systems, rather than mechanical barriers or humans. Well, if there's nobody physically there to stop us, what's the problem? We were, after all, just a dumb pair of sightseeing scooterists…

The wide bridge was surprisingly wet and slippery as we crossed it. On the left we could see the second Bosphorus Bridge, illuminated by LEDs that change colour at regular intervals. To the right was the Sea of Marmara containing a huge, D-Day like flotilla of ships waiting to dock, or move goods onwards into the Black Sea. Ahead lay a 'Welcome to Asia' sign flanked by a massive row of toll-stations. Dean aimed straight for an open toll-gate with a picture of the HGS card above it.

I nearly jumped out of my skin as all hell broke loose. Alarms and flashing lights went berserk to indicate that someone had driven through without a pre-payment card. Unperturbed we carried on a few hundred metres, and turned off at the first exit for a dawn photo-session on another continent. Nobody chased us. So far we were safe.

Ten minutes later we rode back over the bridge, this time passing the 'Welcome to Europe' sign. A traffic police car pottered along the bridge in the hard shoulder. I didn't want to overtake, but they were driving so slowly that we had no choice but to slowly burble past. Thankfully there were no toll booths in this direction so they remained oblivious that we hadn't paid. Soon enough we were off the motorway and in the clear, but why stop there?

At the next traffic lights I suggested that we push our luck a little further by riding to Taksim Square to see if any remnants of the protests existed. I suspected that sticking our unwanted noses into the highly emotive world of Turkish politics was far more likely to rile the police than skipping a toll on our scooters.

Perhaps by good fortune, the whole Taksim Square area was deserted. There was nothing to show for the protests since the 'occupy Gezi' movement had been forcibly removed. Besides the reverberating din of two-stroke scooters bouncing off the buildings, and the presence of the odd armoured police vehicle in the side streets, all was at peace. Istanbul was waking up though, and we needed to get back before every street became constipated with cars.

Less than an hour after setting off I tore back up the hill to the hotel, closely followed by Dean. Even with the engine turned off my scooter makes a characteristic 'ting ting' sound after a good thrash, as the brake components cool and realign. The guys from the hotel were incredulous that we'd been to Asia and back so quickly. Well chaps, these are ICBMs: Inter-Continental Ballistic Motor-scooters.

After a successful mission, Dean and I returned separately to our rooms to catch another hour's sleep, before we left Europe for the second time that day.

Istanbul covers an area of 5,343 square kilometres and is the second most populous city on the planet. Many of the 14 million residents seem resigned to spending their daytime sat in endless traffic jams. Tackling these queues in order leave the city is not an appealing prospect, but thankfully we have another plan. Only a few kilometres from the hotel is a port where we can catch a ferry south west across the Sea of Marmara. Like so much of Turkey our ship is thoroughly modern: a catamaran filled with aircraft-style seats.

Two hours later we arrive back in Asia for the second time that day, in the port of Bandirma, en route to Canakkale for a slice of military history.

Patience is clearly not a natural trait for residents of Istanbul; particularly not the middle-aged man in his brand new Porsche Panamera, who can't stand the fact that bikes are able to get off the ferry before him. He edges forward until his car touches the number plate of a large Japanese Harley-clone belonging to a bodybuilder guy that we've just been chatting to. Clearly the guy with the Porsche has so much money; he thinks he can do what he likes. The bodybuilder doesn't make much fuss, so maybe he can?

On the whole I find Turkish driving standards to be both poor and unpredictable. I decided to be careful with Turkish people in general because I know that they can be stabby. I've made a mental note not to give any drivers the finger because I don't want this road trip to end like the movie Easy Rider.

If any company can be said to have changed the early part of the 21st century, then it is Google. It's difficult to think back to the time when researching anything meant picking up a guide, an encyclopaedia or an atlas. In Istanbul I wondered if the road between Bandirma and Canakkale went through a desert. The answer was simply to pick up my Google tablet, open Google maps and switch to satellite view.

The satellite images revealed a hilly landscape dotted with trees; which is exactly what we found when we disembarked the ferry. What Google Maps doesn't tell you is that the whole region is ferociously windswept on a semi-permanent basis. Canakkale gets on average 260 windy days a year. That's the equivalent of every day except for weekends.

A little wind passing through our perforated jackets was something of a blessing with air temperatures consistently above 35C. Even with that breeze it was so hot that both Sam and Kimberly started to fall asleep on the scooters. As a rider it's easy to tell when your pillion has drifted off. Their head slumps forward and then the crash helmet starts to nudge you in the back. Only a break for iced coffees reenergised the kids sufficiently to complete the journey.

Canakkale sits at the southern tip of a narrow channel called the Dardanelles; which links the Sea of Marmara with the wider Mediterranean. Marmara in turn connects to The Black Sea via the Bosphorus at Istanbul. Such a commanding location made Canakkale a strategically important site for many thousands of years, as the power of empires ebbed and flowed. It was therefore also a jolly good place for a scrap.

In northern Europe we have our own designated fighting arena, known as Belgium. Whenever the British, French, Dutch or Germans fancy having a bloody battle it seems to be the ideal place, particularly if wet fields and muddy trenches are your thing. Canakkale seems to be the Eurasian equivalent, given that it is located only 25km north of the ancient City of Troy where, according to legend, the ancient Greeks spent ten years laying siege to the city all because of a stolen woman. As so often with punch-ups, there always seems to be a woman involved.

If you believe the ancient narrative then the Greeks finally sacked the city after pretending to bugger off, while at the same time leaving a large wooden horse as a gift to the Trojans. There remains some mystery as to why the Trojans accepted a large gift from a sworn enemy, but I believe that the horse was actually addressed to the civilisation next door. The people of Troy, being very neighbourly offered to look after it until the Teuthranians came back from holiday.

Of course the fabled twist was that the hollow horse contained Greek soldiers who snuck out in the night and sacked the city before setting it on fire. Naturally all this has been Hollywoodified in the film Troy, and the horse used in that film is now on display on Canakkale seafront. Sam was slightly disappointed to find that this Trojan horse was actually a fibreglass film prop and not the 3,500 year old original, but then again, kids are notoriously hard to please.

Perhaps marginally less famous but certainly more recent, relevant and costly was the Battle of Canakkale: better known in English-speaking countries as the Gallipoli Campaign. Gallipoli is actually a small town on the opposite side of the straights from Canakkale.

In 1915 the Gallipoli peninsula became the site of a WW1 military clusterfuck that cost at least 100,000 lives, and left half a million casualties. War may be bad, but a pointless and ineptly fought one is hell.

Separated from the fighting by almost a century it is difficult to convey to Sam the full horror of what went on, but the huge cannon mounted on a railway carriage opposite our hotel certainly made an impact, or at least received one. This enormous Turkish artillery piece is supported on an inch-thick steel frame which has been ripped open like a Coke-can stabbed with a biro. To an eleven year old boy with an unhealthy interest in guns, this was not an instrument of death. It was merely an object of immense power that he was permitted to climb on.

At school I successfully managed to get kicked out of history lessons before we reached the interesting and relevant bits on the 20th century. As such I really had no idea what the battle was all about, so I was forced to do a little research.

In essence Gallipoli was a Commonwealth and French military operation aimed at opening a sea route to our Allies in Russia. The Turkish army – which sided with Germany in WW1 – not only fought to prevent the linking of the Allied Western and Eastern fronts, but also to defend their homeland from an invasion that threatened Istanbul.

It is ironic that leaders considered by many to be saviours of their nations – Winston Churchill and Ataturk – were both involved militarily in the Gallipoli campaign, but with very different results. As head of the Admiralty, it was Churchill's bold plan to attack the

Dardanelles and Istanbul in the first place. The initial naval assault was abandoned after losing several ships because the narrow straight was amply defended by coastal guns, torpedoes and mines.

Two months later – with plenty of time for the Turks to prepare defences – an ill-conceived land assault was mounted at several beach landing sites. All quickly became bogged down in the face of fierce and costly Turkish counter-attacks.

Mustapha Kemal Ataturk commanded the 19th division defending the beachhead known as Anzac Bay against mainly Australian and New Zealand troops. He famously inspired his fighters with the following quote:

'Men, I am not ordering you to attack. I am ordering you to die. In the time that it takes us to die, other forces and commanders can come and take our place.'

After eight months, with no obvious means to break the entrenched deadlock, the Allies reluctantly evacuated their forces. As seemed so common in The Great War, the only land actually taken for all this bloodshed would be the soil stuck to the boots of the men who departed.

For Mustapha Kemal the costly victory at Gallipoli was one of the defining moments that saw him establish a new Turkish state in 1923. He subsequently introduced many reforms which saw Turkey become a forward-thinking secular nation. By contrast the humiliating defeat of Gallipoli nearly finished the military and political career of Winston Churchill, were it not for my country's need for a strong leader in the next war. At least the Turkish campaign taught Churchill exactly how *not* to mount an amphibious landing.

*Dean in Asia after our dawn ride over the Bosphorus Bridge.*

*The Lambrettas in Taksim Square, Istanbul.*

# BACK TO EUROPE
## Day 18: Canakkale (Turkey) to Alexandroupoli (Greece)

In the morning after a single night in Canakkale we made our own amphibious assault, crossing the narrow waterway on the car ferry to Eceabat on the Gallipoli side. This channel is the marine equivalent of a motorway: heavy with freight and constantly patrolled by the Turkish Navy. The huge commemorative Turkish flag carved into the hillside on the northern shore made it clear that the area had not forgotten the events of World War 1, but nothing prepared us for what we found immediately off the ferry.

Tarihe Saygi Parki (Respect for History Park) on Eceabat seafront is easily the most moving war memorial I've ever seen. There, in life-size bronzes, is a full trench battle scene with the Turks on one side and Anzacs on the other. In the no-man's land between, lie dead bodies of both sides piled up amidst spent shell casings.

Rather than gloating over their victory, or only being concerned for their own dead, the towering monument in the park depicts all the nationalities that fought together on a single statue, with Ataturk depicted carrying a wounded Australian soldier. It says something about the make-up of young boys that Sam was more moved by the sight of the weapons, than the death and destruction that they represented. Maybe it takes age and wisdom to remove the glamour from combat.

For us the only remaining battle was staying on the road. The windy region of Canakkale lived up to its reputation on our route northeast along the coast. I found it hard to hold my Lambretta in a straight line as the wind tore in from the sea, so I was really proud of Tracy's ability to fight the gale on the Maicoletta. In a section of roadworks we entered a temporary sandstorm which allowed the swirling vortices to become suddenly visible. Sensibly, all our scooters run air filters because to ride in such gritty conditions without one would kill an engine in no time.

At Kesan we turned west and headed for the Greek border crossing near Ipsala; where we stopped to fill both fuel tanks and bellies. Turkey's last surprise pulled into the petrol station behind us with a chug of a single cylinder engine that sounded like it came from a canal barge.

Back in Britain during the 1980s there was a craze for cutting down the bodywork of scooters to the absolute bare functioning minimum. This device was the lorry equivalent. The entire cab was missing, presumably lost along with the license plate and the seats. Instead the old driver sat on cushions, equipped only with a baseball hat and eyebrows that were thicker than his tyre tread. Only when the old fellow and his passenger chuffed leisurely out onto the main road, with their engine firing once every lamp post, did I notice an old lady sat in the flatbed of the truck. This oddball vehicle served as a sharp reminder that while Istanbul may be modern and forward thinking, there are still poor areas of the country that are quite the opposite.

Exiting Turkey was slightly less arduous than entering it, with only four checks (passports, passports and vehicle documents, vehicle documents and finally passports and documents again) required before we could leave. Oddly, Tracy's scooter refused to start using the key between the many checkpoints. Dean and I were forced to run and push-start the Maico in torturous heat, before returning it to Tracy with strict, sweat-laden instructions not to turn it off again.

We pulled up at the last booth where the guy told us that our scooters were horrible noisy things and made us turn them all off. He then checked our documents one final time for good measure. Bastard.

I wondered if his computer would highlight our little indiscretion in crossing the Bosphorus without a toll card, but in the end he waved us on. Tracy's scooter thankfully sparked into life leaving us only to cross the small bridge over the River Potamos. There the flags of

Greece and Turkey fly side by side, like two sworn enemies forced to share a seat on a busy bus.

I made a point of waving at the Turkish sentries as we passed, and they waved back. This in turn forced the bored-looking Greek soldiers on the other side of the bridge to also wave, so as not to look unfriendly.

As EU passport holders, entering Greece was a mere formality and soon we were on a fast two-lane road of thick black tarmac. Suddenly it felt like we were home again, in Western Europe. Little churches replaced mosques.

With the wind now at our backs we made good progress on the motorway to a little hotel built on scrub land near Alexandroupoli's municipal hospital. The out-of-town location didn't matter; only that it had a swimming pool to cool off after our sand-blasting in Turkey.

The irony of that day's ride had not eluded me. We travelled from one country that wanted to join the European Union, but hadn't yet been allowed, and instead entered one that remains within the European Union, but only by the skin of its teeth.

By 2013 Greece was two years into a financial crisis and government austerity programme that saw unemployment rise to 27%. However that summer was proving to be a good one for the tourism industry, as they enjoyed what I call 'the Aldi effect'. The perception in northern Europe was that cash-strapped Greece must be ripe for a deal and therefore a bargain place for a holiday. While Greece remains in the Eurozone, this will never really be true. You might be able to travel there from Germany or France without changing currencies, but equally things cost pretty much the same as they do back home. The bargain holidays of old afforded by different exchange rates will never exist again within the single currency zone.

*Sam with a shell-damaged WW1 gun, Canakkale.*

*Photo session with the horse from the film 'Troy',*
*Canakkale. (Photo: Kim)*

*Mustafa Ataturk depicted carrying a wounded Australian
soldier, Eceabat.*

*Statues portray the horrors of Gallipoli's trench warfare, Eceabat.*

*Strange cut-down truck, Ipsala, Turkey.*

# EVEN HONDA ENGINES HAVE FAULTS
## Day 19: Alexandroupoli (Greece) to Thassos

In the morning things looked promising. The sun was shining as usual, but the wind had dropped and Tracy's scooter started without needing to be pushed. All we had to do was 134km to the ferry port at Keramoti.

You should always be wary when things seem easy.

A few miles from the hotel, at our first petrol stop, my scooter started spewing oil from its crankcase breather pipe. That was not a good sign.

No engine is perfect, and while my Honda CRM motor is highly competent, it does have a known weak link. The two-stroke oil pump, which is driven directly from the crankshaft by plastic gears, is prone to wear in high-mileage engines. One symptom is that the cylinder slowly fills with two-stroke oil if the engine remains un-started for a while. Mine had been like that for about a year: difficult to kickstart after a lay-up and smoking like tyres on a bonfire once you finally got it running. Rather than tackle the problem in advance – as I really had my hands full building the Maico – I simply packed a second-hand oil pump in case of disasters.

The other symptom of a worn-out CRM engine is that the seal on the oil pump drive shaft starts to leak. Consequently the pump then fills the gearbox with two-stroke oil which, once full, leaks out of the gearbox breather pipe.

Sound familiar?

There was nothing for it but to dismantle the engine and fit the other pump.

'How long will it take?' enquired Dean, as helpful as ever.

'About half an hour, but the pump is in a second storage box that I've built into the back of the Maico. Can you take the body off please, so we can get to it?'

By this stage our merry band worked together like a well-oiled machine. Maybe not as well-oiled as my gearbox but certainly not far off. The luggage piled high on the Maicoletta's rear seat required removal at every petrol stop. Tracy dealt with that first before Sam and Dean removed the heavy rear bodywork.

By the time a convoy of 4x4 vehicles pulled into this little garage we had two disassembled scooters spread all over the forecourt. This group of Toyota Land Cruisers and Jeeps all wore Italian number plates, and stickers from previous overland adventures to China and Africa. A couple of drivers recognised the Lambrettas and came over to have a look, but they left us to work without striking up conversation.

Unlike our do-it-the-hard-way vintage scooters, these folks had all the right kit for long distance touring. One even had an accessory that allowed the Land Cruisers' tyre pressures to be altered for sandy terrain while still driving.

The problem with having the hardcore equipment is that you have to do hardcore things to justify owning it; which is fine if you have the time and money to invest. Fair play to this crew though, they were the real deal, not just poseurs who take their off-roaders no further than the nearest supermarket. That sort of behaviour reminds me of obese Britons who don track suits and running trainers to wobble only as far as the local chip shop.

Having worked quickly to swap the pump, drain the excess oil from the gearbox and put the scooters back together, we were on the road before the Italians.

Their big convoy caught and overtook our little convoy on the next section of Greek motorway, while we were travelling at a Dean's maximum velocity. I let them get a little way ahead before opening the throttle, praying that the new oil pump was working, and winding the scooter up to top speed. The 4x4 drivers were either open-mouthed or smiling as Sam and I ripped past them. Being Italian they all knew what a Lambretta was, but you can bet that they weren't used to being overtaken by one on the motorway.

Everything in engineering, and life, is about compromise. Dean's scooter may not be a rocket-ship, but then again it was relatively frugal and he never needed to lay a spanner on it for the entire journey. By contrast Tracy and I had scooters that accelerated like motorcycles. The price of this performance was that we had to frequently adjust, lubricate and check things; particularly the overstressed scooter parts of the equation. That's a cost I don't mind paying; particularly if it leaves other road users shocked or impressed.

There are many ways to skin a cat, but for best results it should always be alive…

On the motorway I considered how smartphones and tablet computers have revolutionised travel in the connected world. With mini tablets now costing less than £50 and free Wi-Fi available in many places, our planet has become a much smaller place.

Organising hotels in advance via the internet each day, probably saved two hours compared to arriving in a town with nothing booked, hunting around and possibly finding somewhere that even cockroaches consider grotty. The old-school alternative would be rigorous research and booking up everything before you start the trip, but then you're stuck with a rigid timetable which can't easily be altered to cater for whims or mechanical breakdowns. Instead, with web access, we could spend 15 minutes on Booking.com and leave knowing not only our exact destination, but also that the hotel came highly recommended.

Hotel reservation apps are like any tool. You need to learn how to get the best out of them: how to pick somewhere in a good location from the maps, how to decipher the promotional blurb and determining which reviews are worthy of attention. Information filtering is an essential skill for the 21st century.

Those who lose out with this new technology are the hotels that either don't take part or have terrible customer reviews. In the past if you had a bad hotel experience there was never really any way to get satisfaction, but web sites featuring reviews have suddenly empowered the customer. Far from low prices equalling inferior service – as they usually do on budget airlines – discounted advance hotel bookings seem to get you better treatment than if you come off the street and paid the going rate. This is a big change. This is consumer power in action.

In our hotel in Alexandroupoli we'd used this technology to arrange the next stage of our trip; a few days holidaying on the island of Thassos where we would celebrate Sam's 12th birthday in style. We'd booked a hotel in the resort town of Limenaria which had excellent reviews, but experience taught us to be careful. We always chose to book a single night in case a hotel turned out to be awful, and then added extra days if we liked it.

We needn't have worried about Thassos.

*Dean and Kim perform the PFJ salute. Splitters!*

*Oil pump replacement in a Greek petrol station. (Photo: Kim)*

*The Maico bodywork must be removed to access the spare*
*Honda CRM oil pump stashed inside.*

# GREEK TRAGEDY
## Days 20 & 21: Thassos

We spent three days in beach holiday mode at the wonderful Samaras Beach hotel in Limenaria, on the southern coast of Thassos. On arrival I mentioned Sam's birthday to Katia – the owner – and the following morning she presented him with a cake for breakfast, especially prepared by her baker husband. Both Sam and Kim were treated to Jetski rides and a parachute trip behind a speedboat. All this took place at a resort a couple of kilometres up the coast. For convenience we rode three-up again, on the enormous bench seat of the Maicoletta, with all our freshly-bought snorkelling gear strapped to the back rack.

On the Greek islands you are told that you shouldn't flush your toilet paper because the narrow waste pipes are prone to blocking. Instead, you are expected to put your used arse-wipes in a specific bin in the bathroom. Personally I find it more likely that the Greeks don't want you flush your bog paper because it then becomes totally obvious where all the sewage goes. Certainly it does once you start swimming through a fog of tiny paper fragments just off the shore of any busy town. The problem with the Mediterranean is that there is very little tide, so anything flushed out into the sea has a tendency to hang about like a bored teenager. My advice is to find a swimming beach away from the town, where the water will be much cleaner.

Our days on Thassos wouldn't merit much mention, were it not for me undermining all the relaxation on our second day, while trying to fix the intermittent starting problem on Tracy's Maicoletta.

Generally small groups tend to get on better when there are an even number of members, but even as a 'five' we'd got to this point with barely any arguments. Some of this was due to Dean's very proactive response to quickly tackle, defuse and solve issues. When it came to the repair of the Maico's electrical problem at the side of the hotel in soaring temperatures, Dean was being as helpful as usual; assisting with the removal of the rear bodywork and fetching the spare battery off his scooter to try. While I worked, he asked questions about the wiring and the function of various unfamiliar electrical components. My problem was that I was trying to logically figure out what was wrong with an electrical system that I'd created and understood, while at the same time fielding questions. In the direct sunlight of 35-degree heat I found Dean's well-intentioned enquiries extremely distracting.

The flash-point came, quite literally, when I had the power wire from the battery in my hand and was told to stop working because the kids had just bought kebabs for lunch. As I looked up, the thick battery cable in my hand touched the motor and a series of cracking sparks hit the engine. After so many miles the unwashed motor was covered in a mist of oil and fuel and was a potential firebomb. With the petrol tank in the same vicinity, that'd wouldn't be a fire you could put out easily.

Mercifully the scooter didn't catch light, but my next thought was to worry whether the sensitive electronic components on this engine would be damaged by such a jolt. Partly in frustration at my own clumsiness and stupidity, I flipped out.

'FUCK OFF, JUST FUCK OFF', I shouted.

Dean looked shocked but ushered the children away helpfully.

'You don't mean me do you?' he said; naive that he'd been a contributing party.

'And you', I replied, bitterly.

Now if you are ever in a similar situation and someone is doing their best to help, then might I suggest that a more suitable reply is: 'Can you give me some space to think this through please?' Telling them to fuck off can cause offence, particularly if the receiving party is not used to foul-mouthed Londoners, for whom that phrase can mean anything from 'are you joking?' through to a recognised opener for extreme violence.

While Tracy helped me to finish rebuilding the Maico – which started perfectly afterwards, possibly due to Dean's input – she made it clear that I'd broken a taboo. The only thing for it was a grovelling apology to Dean and also to Kim, who'd been told to fuck off when all she'd done was to get us some lunch. I hoped that Dean would forgive me in the end, but I wasn't so sure about Kimberly.

This episode put a dampener on our last day on Thassos, to the point where Dean and Kim considered doing the last part of the journey on their own. I hoped it wouldn't come to that.

*Engine heat melted the casing of the Maico's intact fuse.*
*(Photo: Tracy)*

# GRECIAN 2000
## Day 22: Thassos to Thessaloniki

We got up early and rushed to catch the infrequent ferry to Kavala on the mainland. Thankfully after a night of contemplation the mood within the group had improved. Everyone agreed that we should complete the journey together. However I resolved to keep my playful nature locked safely in the doghouse for a while.

The ferry journey gave me a chance to reflect.

Cue some wobbly video effects used to signify a scene from an earlier time…

Greece and I go back a long way; to 1989 in fact when I first rode out on a Lambretta chopper in an ultimately doomed quest to reach the pyramids by scooter. In the end my finances dwindled and Athens – only a ferry ride from Egypt – was as far as I ever managed. One thing I did discover in Athens, due to a mechanical breakdown, was that Lambrettas were still being used as transport in the major Greek cities. More importantly, spares were freely available during a period when Italians considered the brand to be dead.

I'd ridden into Athens after giving my mate Damien a lift from the holiday island of Corfu, where he'd found me a job working for a beach water-sports company. The job was torture; several weeks in the sun being paid to fit lifejackets to bikini-clad girls.

Damien was a fellow member of my first scooter club: 'The Knights Who Say Ni!', named after some ridiculous characters from Monty Python's Quest for the Holy Grail. He had been working on Corfu as a travel rep, but while I was there he was suddenly made redundant. Sensing an opportunity, I jacked my beach job and offered to take him wherever he wanted to go, preferably in an Egypt-bound direction.

We arrived in Athens with all Damien's worldly possessions strapped to the chopper's 'cissy bar' backrest, and then the rear wheel fell off the scooter. Literally. At best you might call this an inconvenience, but the Lambretta rear hub is a strange mechanical fit of cone and splines. When these become damaged the hub is basically useless. You aren't going anywhere unless you can find a replacement hub.

Lambretta hubs remain a weak link in the design to this day. Even with the power of the internet, mobile phones, credit cards and rapid international courier services, a broken hub might still take a couple of days to replace. For that precise reason, Dean carried a brand new hub on our current trip, bolted inside the spare wheel on his rear rack.

Back in the 1980s however, Damien and I had none of those luxuries. All we could do was bodge the damaged wheel back on and push the heavily laden chopper around the streets of Athens to try and find help.

Amazingly we did find help in the form of a hovel-like workshop where an old man was repairing a customer's Lambretta on its side, and throwing the old worn-out parts to the back of the shop. There they formed a scrap steel tsunami that looked at any moment like it might wash the mechanic out of the door, and onto the street. He didn't have a hub, well not a good one, but he did take us around the corner to a building several stories high which was literally rammed with brand new Italian-made Lambretta spares. This was despite the fact that manufacturers Innocenti stopped making scooters and parts in 1973.

These fortuitous events seemed so unlikely, particularly when I relayed them in a series of articles in Scootering Magazine that I sometimes wondered if they actually happened, and those places really did exist. However, such positive experiences at the tender age of 21 shaped my thinking. They are precisely the reason that I have enough faith, confidence, arrogance or optimism, call it what you will, to embark on so many silly adventures riding unsuitable scooters.

Experience had taught me that if you put in a reasonable amount of preparation then 'it will probably be all right'. Even when things don't go to plan there are character-building lessons in overcoming obstacles. As Esther Rantzen would repeat, through Bee Gees-topping gnashers; 'That's Life!'

Ironically it was Dean who confirmed that those mythical Athens shops did exist, when he and several other British Lambretta specialists embarked on parts buying armadas to Greece in the 1990s. They found both businesses still trading, just as I had described them.

Subsequently Dean has continued to scour Greece for scooters and parts and it's one of his many Greek contacts that we planned to meet at our next stop off, in the second city of Thessaloniki. Ironically Mustafa Ataturk – the founder of modern Turkey – was born there in 1881, when the city was still under Ottoman rule and known as Selanik.

Even riding from the ferry port at Kavala we noticed that the Greeks still seem to make considerable effort to keep old vehicles on the road, where in more affluent countries they are simply scrapped and replaced with the latest thing. As if to emphasise this point we spotted an old couple at a set of traffic lights aboard a red Heinkel Tourist. Both of them wore hats rather than crash helmets and the wife sat side-saddle, leaning against a beach chair on the back rack with a folded parasol resting on her lap.

The Tourist was another large German luxury scooter produced through the late 1950s and early 1960s, and therefore very much a historic rival of Tracy's Maicoletta. With a 175cc four-stroke engine, the Heinkel Tourist is famed for reliability. As such it wouldn't surprise me to find out that this one had been in use pretty much continuously since it was new, and travelled the equivalent of several laps of the planet. Half a century later, there it was, still dutifully transporting its owners to the beach.

I wonder how many of the scooters and cars sold today will still be in daily use in fifty years time? Probably none. I expect that future generations will consider burning fossil fuels in vehicle engines as abhorrent as slavery.

Dean's contact in Thessaloniki is called Dimitrios, and he rode his Lambretta SX200 round to meet us at our hotel. We'd booked the only one in the city with a roof-top swimming pool. By the time Dimitrios rolled up we'd well and truly lowered the tone of the unbearably pompous pool and bar area. Swimming for us is about noisy splashing rather than delicate and silent breast stroke. Whatever couth is, it appears we are without it.

Dimitrios is a good laugh, and a confirmed anglophile. He lived in Coventry and Brighton in his youth, before being dragged back home to fulfil his national service obligation in the army. Dimitrios never returned to Britain to complete his studies and has worked in various fields while fixing scooters on the side ever since. His smart Lambretta is customised very much in the 1960s British street-racer style with a low sports seat, spotlights on the legshields and a huge Smiths speedometer moulded into the headset.

That evening we rode together to Thessaloniki's seafront, to hook up with fellow Lambretta owners Spyros, Manos and Helena, before blasting back through the busy city streets around midnight. Here in the city centres, Greek police travel around 2-up on middleweight motorcycles, offering the ultimate in agility and fast response in a built up area. We were followed unknowingly by just such a pair, while we noisily thrashed the scooters away from the traffic lights, but they didn't bat an eyelid at our boisterous riding. Clearly there are bigger fish to fry in Greece's second city.

One effect of the Greek government trying to claw back the national debt to cover their own failings, and those of greedy bankers, is they have driven many transactions underground. The last thing cash-strapped people are willing to do is pay more tax, so many

Greek transaction now seem to be a mix of official and unofficial cash payments. Certainly I noticed that the till receipt I was given for one purchase on Thassos showed a figure far lower than I'd actually paid. It made no difference to me, so I didn't say anything.

What people in Britain probably don't appreciate are the lengths that governments will go to, in struggling economies like Italy or Greece, in order to counter this black market economy. Certainly Italy has its own financial police force, which has the power to stop anyone leaving a store and demand to see the receipt for their last purchase. In recent years Guardia di Finanza officers have descended on major cities, stopping anyone in a high-end sports car and enquiring how they managed to afford such a vehicle. Let's be straight, these police are not really looking for drug dealers, they are simply looking for tax avoiders. If you were a criminal who declared a healthy income and paid a respectable amount of tax then presumably that was ok? After all, it was the crime of tax avoidance that finally got Al Capone sent to prison, not the gangland massacres he instigated.

*Tracy on the overloaded Maicoletta.*

*1989: Damien with my Lambretta chopper in Athens.*

*1960s Heinkel Tourist, Kavala, Greece.*

*Riding behind Spyros and Dimitrios, Thessaloniki, Greece.*

*Manos, Spyros and Dimitrios with their Lambrettas.*

# YOU TAKE THE HIGH ROAD
## Day 23: Thessaloniki (Greece) To Monodendri

After a late night we didn't manage to leave the hotel in the morning as sharply as we should. Instead we ate a leisurely breakfast watching middle-class Italian pensioners ravaging the free buffet, with plates piled like scale models of Pisa's leaning tower. Many rolls and pastries were slipped slyly into handbags. It's funny how the most generous areas of society seem to be the poor and the ultra-rich, but those in the middle, who are comfortably-off but aspire to be rich, can be the tightest bastards on the planet. I wondered if these old Italians really could not afford their next meal, or if they were just stocking up out of sheer greed because it was free. Maybe they were actually skint. Keeping up with the Joneses can be an expensive game.

Our destination for the night was another hotel with a pool, but this time 300km west and set high in the Pindus mountain range above Ioannina. There – the guide books told us – lay the Vikos Gorge; apparently the deepest gorge in the world for its width.

The only sensible way to get out of Thessaloniki was on the motorway, which quickly developed into a boring slog in astronomic temperatures, without even the comfort of a breeze. We rode together at 55mph on the flat road around the top of the Thermaic Gulf. At that speed, distant Mount Olympus (and its famous camera factory) appeared to get no nearer.

Occasionally when Dean approached a lorry of similar speed I pulled just ahead, allowing him to grasp the Invisible Tow Rope (ITR) and increase top speed just enough to creep past the truck. The ITR is actually the slipstream effect as used by Tour de France cyclists. Slipstreaming allows a closely following rider to use roughly 30% less energy than the leader, even when travelling at the same speed. In our case, the hole my scooter made in the air allowed Dean's to go slightly faster on the same amount of power.

The last part of this manoeuvre is the trickiest, because every lorry creates a massive invisible bow-wave which is hard to push past with evenly-matched performance. You might not be able to see it, but you can certainly feel its effect slowing down the scooter when pulling alongside the driver's cab, particularly if you have car drivers impatiently tailgating you. Having a more powerful scooter to slipstream meant that Dean and Kim had enough surplus speed to break through this barrier and complete the overtake. Teamwork in action.

It was a real disappointment to witness that Greeks on the mainland didn't seem to care about their environment. Up on the plains between the mountains, way out of sight of the tourists, they've hidden some of the ugliest coal-fired power stations this side of Nottingham. Many times we came across picturesque vistas spoiled by rubbish that had been fly-tipped down the side of a beautiful mountain. What a criminal waste.

Dean found the motorway monotony as hard going as quicksand, so we pulled off into the town of Kozani for lunch, with the intention to take a northern route on minor roads to reach our destination. As we sat down to eat, a middle-aged guy on a Vespa ETS pulled up to photograph our scooters. He was a member of the large Vespa Club of Kozani and spoke reasonable English, so we quizzed him about our options. He explained that our chosen route, which ran close to the Albanian border, was very slow and twists constantly through mountains that are 1.5km tall. I liked the sound of it, as did Dean, but I could sense that Tracy, who was overheating in the relentless sun, and would rather just get to our destination. Certainly she did not want to risk riding on unlit mountain roads when dusk approached.

Our alternatives were to take the motorway for 140km, or use the minor mountain road alongside it. The parallel minor road doubled-back so often that it added 40km to the distance from point to point.

With the deciding votes left to the kids, the mere mention of a pool at the hotel saw the majority elect in favour of the shortest, fastest route. Damn the Greeks and their ideas on democracy!

Pretty soon we were back on the motorway and climbing barren mountains via long tunnels and sweeping viaducts, with Dean far behind us. That morning he'd woken with a sore back, and I could feel his pain. Having suffered in the past with a herniated disc, I now wear a supportive kidney belt for long rides, but I was happy to donate this to the cause. His need was greater than mine.

Picking up such an injury on a long tour, on a cramped scooter with insufficient suspension travel, is something that really worries me. For Dean, sitting in the same position on the motorway with Kimberly falling asleep in the heat behind him, it was purgatory. As such, he elected to leave the motorway and take the twisty scenic road.

Dean's detour meant that we arrived separately in Monodendri after a long, spectacular climb from the beautiful lakeside city of Ioannina. We arrived with just enough time for Sam to jump in the pool before the sun set behind the hotel, and the chill of our altitude became apparent. Tracy's scooter – parked on the road in this small village – attracted the attention of a fit looking couple who we noticed taking photos of it.

It turned out that Nikos Spanos was the Greek importer for LML: an Indian clone of the Vespa. He is also a former motorcycle journalist who knew several of my Greek friends from Athens. As we talked, I could feel the world below my feet shrinking just a little bit more.

Some time later Dean and Kimberly arrived, full of tales about the wonderful road they had detoured onto, and gushing about how they had seen warning signs about bears in the area. Considering that I would have preferred to take the scenic route myself, this news was not really what I wanted to hear.

Dean had also visited a friend who ran a scooter shop in Ioannina and arranged to meet him for lunch the following day, before heading to the ferry. Instead, I had other plans hatched over a substandard moussaka in the hotel restaurant, which was cold in the middle, like my heart.

I wanted to squeeze one extra country into our agenda at the last minute, with a whistle-stop visit to Albania. I reasoned that we were only 50km from the border so it would be rude not to visit, if only for a coffee. Tracy was less enthusiastic, not so much because of isolated Albania's constant bad press, but simply because we were now so close to the ferry back to Italy, that she didn't want to take any unnecessary risks. Dean had only just managed to squeeze us onto the boat travelling 'deck class' thanks to a contact at the ferry company. That week was perhaps the busiest of the whole summer with millions of Northern European tourists all trying to get home in time for work and the end of the school holidays. We couldn't afford to miss that ferry for exactly the same reasons.

In Tracy's mind I, rather selfishly, wanted to double our riding distance for the day simply to cross the border into another former communist state, just to say we'd been there. Not only that, but we'd have do this extra distance without the security of a third scooter, because Dean had promised Kimberly a morning of shopping in Ioannina before his lunch appointment.

'It'll be all right', I reassured my long-suffering wife, without any real certainty, only a feeling that it would be.

*Kim minding the bears, Greece. (Photo: Dean)*

*The statue of the Zagori woman, near Monodendri, Greece.*

# ALBANIAN WHISTLE-STOP
## Day 24: Monodendri (Greece) To Igoumenitsa

In the morning, before going our separate ways, we had one more target to reach together. That was to continue riding the narrow road 10km onwards from our hotel in Monodendri, to the dead end at the top of the Vikos Gorge. As the road snaked higher rock formations on either side grew ever more psychedelic. Eventually we entered the 'Stone Forest' where fine layers of rock are stacked upon one another, and carved by the weather into odd, loaf-like structures.

The road eventually ran out, which left us 100-metres of stony path to walk before reaching the viewing platform on the cliff-edge. Below lay an open wound in the earth: a scar carved a kilometre down by tributaries of the River Voidomatis. The sheer sides of the gorge are entirely unfenced which can lead to feelings of vertigo in even the bravest souls. Sam though, bounded around confidently like a mountain goat.

I was awestruck not only by the gorge, but also the barren feel of the whole Pindus National Park. This is a genuine use of the word awe, not the overused American hyperbole that causes erectile dysfunction in powerful words like 'awesome'.

If you come, as I do, from a country where reaching the tallest peak requires only a stout pair of walking boots, then proper mountain scenery can't help but stir the soul. I'm used to landscapes that could easily be viewed through a letterbox, from the highest hill to the ground beneath your feet. In the Alps or the Vikos Gorge it is not sufficient to move your eyeballs up and down to take it all in, you have to move your whole head. When nature achieves earthworks this impressive, it almost deserves a round of applause.

If Vikos wasn't breathtaking enough, when we stopped to take photos of the scooters overlooking the mountains, we could clearly hear the howl of a wolf pack as they hunted in a tree-covered landscape far below. There is something incredibly raw and primeval about this place.

After the photo session we went our separate ways: Dean and Kim into Ioannina, while Tracy, Sam and I cracked on the 50km or so for Albania. The road to the border seemed to be constantly patrolled by a stream of beaten-up looking Greek police cars, presumably used as a token gesture to stem the massive flow of illegal immigrants. The phrase 'pissing in the wind' springs to mind.

No less than half a million Albanians have moved to Greece since the 1990s, mostly for economic reasons, but the Albanian mafia have ensured that the border remains permanently leaky for anyone keen to get into European Schengen zone.

We reached the border to be greeted by a short queue of vehicles waiting to get into Albania. Entry required a document check and passport stamp showing that we had travelled by scooter. It then dawned that our riding insurance didn't cover us for Albania, and we are supposed to pay £13 each for a 'Green Card'. Once we finally made our way through all the checkpoints Tracy took one look at the even longer queue to get out of Albania, and pointed out that we really did not have time to go any further. Not if we were to meet Dean again and make the ferry that same night.

Instead, we elected to skip the expense and paperwork of a Green Card, and simply grabbed a coffee at the border bar before turning around again. This really was a flying visit.

The Albanian local currency is the Lek, of which we had none, but the barman was willing to accept Euros. From the bar I could see a group of fat-bummed ebony Africa ladies who'd been arrested and were being escorted into a secure compound. It's obvious that this particular border is a hotbed of organised crime, but the business here is human trafficking, not the theft of oddball vintage scooters. As such we parked them unlocked outside the busy cafe, but always within sight.

Tracy noticed from the TV in the bar – which was blaring an Albanian news channel – that we had crossed time zones again, moving back one hour to the same zone as Italy. But we were about to cross back into Greece again. Not really worth resetting our watches for the length of time it takes to drink an Albanian cappuccino.

The queue to get back into Greece was huge and moved like treacle. The temptation to push to the front was equally massive, but everyone sat in cars was baking in the heat like we were. I was tentative because I didn't know if Albanians are aware of 'the rules' about bikes being given carte blanche to go ahead. Then a young couple on a Greek-plated superbike then turned up, and totally circumvented the queue. He parked up, walked to the passport booth and was dealt with promptly. More importantly nobody harassed him, so we elected to do the same.

Pretty soon we were back in Greece and heading to the beautiful centre of Ioannina for our appointment with Dean's friend who runs a classic scooter shop called 'Vintage Scooters'.

We were warmly greeted by the shop owner while Dean conducted the formal introduction.

'Sticky, this is Harry', said Dean

'Actually my name is Aris', replied Aris, in immaculate English.

'Yes, whatever you say, Harry', mocked Dean.

It was clear to everyone that Aris was not going to shake the name Harry, and protesting would only make it worse. Instead he concentrated on being the perfect host and ordered in a round of iced coffees.

The shop, which was only opened in February of 2013, was small but superbly turned out. It contained several used Vespas and Lambrettas as well as a lovely Heinkel Tourist that Aris had restored for his father. Ironically, the only new scooters on sale were LML's look-a-likes of the Vespa PX, imported by Nikos whom we met by chance in Monodendri the day before. The world beneath my Salomon hiking boots shrank once more.

All too soon it was time to leave Ioannina and head for the ferry port in Igoumenitsa which is 78km away by the new motorway, or 93km away via the old road through the mountains. It was no contest, with the longer route not only taking us through some of the most scenic mountain passes of the whole trip, but also being largely deserted due to the presence of the fast but dull new highway.

The twisty mountain roads were impossibly picturesque: the sort of involving tarmac sinews used for supercar sequences on Top Gear. It's amazing that this knotted intestine of a street was the main route through northern Greece from the Italian ferry ports, before the motorway was completed. The road certainly wouldn't have been so much fun if it were full of lorries and caravans.

We arrived at the ferry port of Igoumenitsa to find it full of lorries and caravans. In fact the car park contained every form of transport from pedal cycles to Italian-plated supercars. The cultural make-up of the foot-passengers gathered at the port was equally diverse: from ethnically dressed Caucasian hippy women in MC Hammer trousers to whole families of Romany gypsies and every other race in between.

We were ushered to one corner of the busy quayside along with numerous motorcyclists, many of whom were returning to Western Europe after extensive touring holidays. As I gazed across the wide expanse of vehicles waiting to board, it seemed that there was no way we could all possibly fit on this ferry, even if it arrived empty.

It wouldn't. Igoumenitsa was the ferry's second stop, having set off from Patras already half-full with returning holidaymakers. Dean's ferry company contact clearly wasn't joking about us being lucky to get on board, even if it meant slumming it in 'Deck Class' for the princely sum of 350 Euros one-way for two scooters and three people.

Dean was gutted not to get a cabin, but it didn't bother me at all. I still harboured rose-tinted memories of my ferry ride back to Ancona in 1989 with the Japanese hippy girl I'd offered a lift to in Athens, after Damien flew to America in search of new adventures.

Back then Mami and I were utterly broke, without even sufficient petrol money to get my Lambretta back to England. Despite this I was full of adventure and optimism. We spent an exciting night on the crystal-smooth Adriatic, lying with my sleeping bag unfurled on the steel deck and staring at the stars. In the daytime Mami took out a large drawing pad and produced caricatures of our fellow passengers on the ship. By the time we disembarked in Ancona she'd sold several, and earned just enough petrol money to get us to London.

With those youthful experiences still etched into my mind some 24 years later, I resolved to show my wife and son the magic of a night at sea, sleeping under the twinkling panorama of a moonlit sky. As a bonus we would be able to do Deck Class in luxury thanks to the sleeping bags and air mattresses that Tracy's Maico had carried, unused, for our entire trip.

Sadly the loading process was slower than a slug with learning difficulties. We had to wait while Bulgarian lorry drivers made the job of reversing a big rig into a narrow space look effortless. Eventually it became clear that the bikes were only going to fit on last, in any remaining gaps between other vehicles. As such we allowed the kids to go ahead onto the ship and find a prime spot, while we chatted with fellow two-wheeled tourists. Friendliest of this bunch were Udo and Michaela Staleker, a middle-aged couple from central Germany who used the school holidays from their jobs as headmasters to ride a BMW and a KTM to Iran. Udo's enthusiasm and descriptive language shone through, so it was little surprise to find that he was a fellow writer. Stories about their adventures can be found in German magazine Tourenfarhrer (touring rider).

I wondered how Michaela had managed as an empowered woman (literally) in strictly Islamic Iran, but apart from the heat and the lunacy of the traffic in the cities they'd had no problems. Udo's summary was that Iran as a nation gets a bad press, but they found the people on the street very friendly and helpful.

I'm not surprised by this news. My personal belief is that in any place or lifestyle there will be a proportion of people that you'll get on with, and a section that you won't. The proportion of people you dislike – let's call it the Dickhead Ratio for convenience – is not altered so much by where you go, or what sections of society you meet. The proportion of dickheads is primarily set by you, and your tolerance level of other humans.

If you have a low level of tolerance of different lifestyles, and think that most people in your home country are dickheads, then guess what, when you travel abroad or enter a different culture, you'll probably find that a large proportion of the people you meet there are dickheads too. Not because they are dickheads, just because that's where you've set the bar.

On the other hand, if you are willing to make allowances for the failings of others, and get along with 90% of people, then this will probably be true anywhere in the world. In many ways having an optimistic and open outlook makes this a self-fulfilling prophecy. People are far more likely to be hostile or react badly if they believe you are judging them. However if you are honest, sincere and forgiving of their idiosyncrasies, then they are far more likely to be friendly and forgiving of yours. Much of this is transmitted in body language; the often subconscious codes that are used to make an initial assessment of someone.

Naturally the Dickhead Theory does have its exceptions. It only applies to peace-time, and where people haven't been pre-programmed by their upbringing, religion, job or national identity to hate, rob or hurt you. In every case it is wise to hope for the best but prepare for the worst.

As the ferry departed I was vindicated. All of the vehicles did not fit onto the ship. Several cars whose owners had valid ferry tickets were left sitting on the quayside. I can imagine that they were not best pleased, but for the bike riders who squeezed on in the gaps between other vehicles it meant relief. We were on our way home, on time.

The crew of the ferry had a very strange Edwardian attitude to their customers, probably as a result of everyone from gypsies to Ferrari-driving rock stars all being cooped up together inside the same metal hull for 16 hours. The stewards seemed intent on preserving a class system based entirely on money, and how much of it you had to spend.

When Tracy and I finally found our way to the lounge bar to meet Dean and the kids we were refused entry, simply on the basis that we were carrying waterproof bags containing our sleeping gear. The little Greek steward clearly had us marked down as Deck Class scum, therefore in his mind the deck is where we should remain. It probably didn't help that I was wearing a grubby white Sex Pistols-style T-shirt depicting our Queen wearing 3-D glasses, above the word 'Splendid' in ransom-note lettering.

Thus within two minutes of being on board we entered our first argument with the crew. I don't take kindly to being looked down on, particularly not by people unable to do so without the aid of a stepladder.

The steward told us to go away with our bags.

We told him that we wanted a coffee with our kids, and we had nowhere safe to stow the luggage.

He told us to take the baggage away because the bar was for upper class customers.

The stalemate was finally breached by hiding our bags behind a billboard in the lounge and sitting down to order a coffee. Clearly in the mind of this pompous little twerp, this space was reserved for people who could afford cabins. What he didn't appreciate was that this group of dirty scooter scum might well have taken a cabin if there had been any available. Instead, with what we'd saved by going Deck Class, we decided to go for an 'a la Carte' meal with all the trimmings. I wanted to do this not only because it was a better eating option than a tepid buffet, but also as a massive 'up yours' to the judgemental Greek dwarf. He toured the restaurant several times during our meal, eyeing us suspiciously while I made great play of checking the wine list and tucking the napkin into my dirty punk t-shirt.

What's that, you'd like a tip?

Never wipe your arse with a hedgehog…

Our fine dining meant we were late to doss down for the night, so the prime spots had all gone. Unlike the smooth crossing in 1989, this time all the outside decks were very windy. Even so, there were groups of kids laid out under duvets on double-thickness airbeds, fast asleep despite the blustery conditions. We left Dean and Kim, who planned to crash out in the lounge bar, and wandered around looking for somewhere better. Entire Balkan families had occupied all the spaces below the stairs, leaving few other indoor areas available. When we tried to settle in a stairwell, crew members quickly arrived and moved us on.

At the back of the boat was an open deck and a bar semi-covered by a Perspex roof. Here, some savvy travellers had erected pop-up tents, but there would be little rest for them as a travelling band playing gypsy folk music had taken over the bar area. The band were getting stuck in to both their set, and drinks bought for them by other travellers. The party looked set to continue for a long time.

Eventually I found a great spot two decks higher up in a recess at the back of the boat. There, all of our luggage could be safely stored and we could sleep out of the wind. I discovered later why nobody else occupied this prime real estate, when what felt like warm snow-flakes landed on me. We were directly under the trailing plume of soot emitting from the funnels, and our camping mats and sleeping bags were all dotted black with flakes of soot. What the hell, once you're dirty you might as well carry on. Eventually all three of us fell asleep.

*Larking about in the Stone Forest near Monodendri.*

*Entering Albania.*

*Outside (don't call me) Harry's scooter shop, Ioannina, Greece.*

*The old road to Igoumenitsa.*

*Mami with my Lambretta chopper in Greece back in 1989.*

*Waiting for the ferry to dock.*

# WORSE THINGS HAPPEN AT SEA
## Day 25: Adriatic Sea to Borghi (Italy)

At around 2a.m Tracy nudged me awake and I immediately felt the sensation of very fine rain on my face. Stroboscopic sky illuminations warned that this was just a prelude. The ship was sailing into a severe thunderstorm, and we needed to get under cover very quickly.

We were not the only ones to feel the rain. All the kids, hippies and other travellers that were scattered around the outside decks now made a beeline for any space inside, only for the Nazi ship stewards to try to fend people away from the precious areas of the ship that they had pledged to defend. Every stairwell eventually became crowded with bodies, as well as the entire floor of the discotheque.

We tried sleeping with many others in the corridor outside the ferry's gift shop, but it was just too busy and brightly lit. As soon as a crusty fellow lay down nearby and started to snore, I'd had enough. Sam and I left Tracy trying to doze through the din, while we toured the boat in search of a better nest. We found Dean and Kimberly asleep on the floor in a hallway where they'd crashed out, after being ejected from the lounge bar by the grumpy bar-stewards.

Our reconnaissance mission located an empty space that looked perfect for three weary travellers. Through a window we spotted a chained-off VIP section of the discotheque, which consisted of a small spiral staircase leading up to a totally deserted viewing lounge. Bingo!

I smuggled Sam under the chain and told him to wait in the VIP area while I fetched his mum.

Just as Tracy and I started to sneak up the stairs, a crew member caught us.

'No sleep there, come down.'

'My son is asleep up there', I replied in a mixture of tiredness and frustration.

'Not permitted', he tried again

'My son is asleep up there', I repeated, slowly.

If he wanted to get into a noisy argument then I was prepared to give him one, but this would mean waking around 60 people littering the floor in the disco, who would probably have little sympathy for a jobsworth steward.

I've never been one to blindly accept rules if they make no sense. We weren't stopping any VIPs from using that area. It was the middle of the night and they were all tucked up in cabins, so I couldn't see the problem.

The steward could sense that I was low on patience. He decided that, in the interests of an easy life, it was probably better to pretend he hadn't seen me. He wandered off leaving us to creep upstairs to our own private space, for a few precious hours sleep.

There's no way to dress it up: ferries are shit, particularly long crossings in rough weather. By 7a.m the storm had passed, the sun was out and everyone in the disco was rousing. It wasn't long before we were ejected from our hiding place by the naval Gestapo, only to join the army of the undead wandering around in a sleep-deprived daze, counting the hours until we docked in Italy. The concept of boarding a ship for fun fills me with horror. A cruise is just time trapped aboard a slightly posher ferry.

Tiredness took its toll when we finally docked in Ancona. Dean's scooter was parked on a different deck, and I clearly remember arranging to meet him in the first petrol station off the ferry. However, after refuelling and sitting around for half an hour, I finally phoned him, only to find that he had been waiting for us just outside the ferry port. I am aware that limited sleep makes for short fuses, so I subdued my overwhelming desire to take the piss.

The only sensible route to get back to our starting place, at Dean's shop in the hills near Rimini, was to use the motorway. Here at last we were faced with some ominous black clouds that look like they meant business, however Dean was in no mood to stop and don waterproofs for the first time in almost 2,800 miles. A few drops of rain did fall, but we eventually outran the gathering storm, even at the speed of an overloaded Indian Lambretta.

My enduring memory of our return to Italy was seeing Kimberly dancing like a lunatic on the back of her dad's scooter, as we raced up the final few kilometres into the hills. It had been over three weeks since she'd seen her mum and sister, so I understood the excitement, but for us it wasn't the same. We had done our riding as a complete family unit, so there were no relatives to greet us.

While Sam joined in the pillion dancing this was not our home, nor the end of our journey; just the end of the scooter section. Despite meeting up with our Italian friends for a meal that night we felt little elation, only deflation that the ride was over. All that remained was a two-day sprint back to England in the van, in order to be back in time for the routine of work and school. Real life extended a single bony finger and beckoned.

*Pop-up tents: the smart way to 'deck class'.*

*Sleeping 'deck class' in a thunderstorm.*

*Dean and Kim's sleeping arrangements on the boat to Ancona.*

# A TALE OF TWO HOMECOMINGS
## Days 26 & 27: Italy to England

On the drive back through Germany we spotted Udo and Michaela on their motorcycles in a motorway service area. They'd stopped overnight with a friend in Northern Italy and were now not far from home. Seeing them reminded me of a conversation we had on the ferry about kids today, and their attitude to touring and adventure.

When I was at school, being taught by someone who'd seen the world on two-wheels would have been inspirational. By contrast Udo said that not only are his students disinterested in his adventures, they are disinterested in owning bikes or cars.

In the internet age you no longer need to physically move in order to contact your friends. In fact it's often easier to interact with them if you are stationary because texting is difficult while riding or driving. The burning of fossil fuels in vehicles that once enabled us to meet new people, is now a hindrance to youngsters in connecting with their friends. I worry that we are the last of the petrol generation.

Travelling the information super-highway can never replace doing it in real life though. A screen still can't convey the tastes, smells and sounds of Istanbul, the relief of jumping into the sea after a long ride, or even the feel of a place that you can only pick up with a trained sixth sense. Without face-to-face interaction you cannot learn or practice all the important nuances of human body language.

To sit at home and not experience the world around you is to massively miss out on all it has to offer. At the very least, touring makes great material for creating envy amongst your Facebook friends.

After a night in a hotel near the German-French border we drove the last stretch to the Eurotunnel at Calais. When I rode the same route back from Ancona in 1989 with Mami on the pillion seat of my

Lambretta chopper, Britain was still a true island with no physical connection to the continent.

When the Channel tunnel building project began I was not exactly in favour, but once I tried the Eurotunnel my opinion changed. No more slow, wallowy ferries for me, just a fast, efficient moto-rail service to cover the final 26 miles to our sceptred isle.

Except, on our return, the Eurotunnel service was neither fast nor efficient. A technical fault in one of the two tunnels provided a two hour delay, though, to be fair, the company did later reimburse us for this inconvenience.

It always feels odd when, still on French soil, we must conduct a check with UK passport control to access our 'Promised Land'. The right-wing newspapers will tell you that is how every Romanian or Bulgarian views England. Maybe when you see Kent's countryside in the sunshine it appears that way, but scratch the surface to the derelict high streets and it's soon clear that no roads in Britain are paved with gold. Certainly the pristine mountainsides of Germany, Switzerland or Austria look more like Nirvana to me than London; with its permanent umbrella of pollution.

After a short chat with someone from UK Border Agency, and a quick check in the back of our van for unwanted immigrants, we were free to board the train to Britain.

Our return this time was markedly different to the end of my Lambretta adventure in 1989, when Mami and I disembarked the ferry from Ostend in the early hours of the morning.

After meeting me in that Athens youth hostel, Mami sold her camera to fund her ferry tickets, making an irreversible commitment to our journey. Then she travelled over 1,200 miles from Greece on the back of an uncomfortable Lambretta chopper, trusting me and my riding based only on first impressions. She was maybe 30 years old at the time and travelling the world on her own. To this day I can't work out if she was brave, foolhardy, naive or simply optimistic.

Whatever it was, I certainly admired her spirit.

'Are you and this woman in a relationship' asked the female Immigrations officer when Mami showed her Japanese passport in Dover.

'Not really', I replied honestly, 'she's just a friend'.

This was indeed the truth, though I had been tempted to indulge in some Anglo-Japanese relations, in the two nights we had shared under canvas together. What stopped me was that I had a girlfriend in East London who I hadn't seen for six weeks.

'Would you like to wait over there sir, while we ask the lady a few questions?' enquired the officer.

By now it was around 4a.m and I'd only slept for about an hour on the ferry. I would not like to wait, but then again that was not really a question. It was an instruction, dressed in the transvestite uniform of a question.

After another hour, during which time I was given a slightly confusing interview, a second immigrations officer appeared. This one sported the same talent for maltreating the English language.

'I'm afraid', he began, when in fact he was not afraid of anything, 'that we have decided not to let your travelling companion enter the United Kingdom. She does not have a work visa and she has very little money. It is our understanding that you do not have any plans to fund her visit, so she will have no option but to work illegally. We have therefore decided to put her on the next ferry back to Belgium.'

My jaw dropped open like a broken glove-box. I was in shock. It never occurred to me that they might not let Mami into the UK, but now that they hadn't, what were my options? Was it worth changing my statement and saying that we were a couple? It was probably a bit too late for that.

While I was waiting in the ferry terminal I'd chatted to a guy who told me not to mess with Customs and Immigration.

'They've got more powers than the police', he warned. 'They can investigate your bank accounts and bust down your door whenever they like.'

In the end I had no choice. I kicked over the engine of my

Lambretta and rode through the dawn to see my girlfriend. I didn't realise until I arrived at her flat in London, that I still had one of Mami's bags strapped to my scooter. It took many months before Mami managed to contact me so I could return her bag, by which stage she'd got a job fruit-picking in Holland.

The relationship I returned to was rekindled for a short while, right up until the point where I mentioned that I'd given a Japanese girl a lift home from Greece. Despite my assurances that no impropriety took place, I don't think I was ever trusted again, and that relationship broke down soon afterwards.

In a roundabout way, bringing Mami back on my scooter had a major impact on my life, because not long after getting dumped on my return from Greece I got together with Tracy, who I've been with ever since. She not only became my beloved wife and the mother of a fine son, but she's also the sort of girl who's up for unusual suggestions. Suggestions like building her a Frankenstein scooter, so we could all ride together to Istanbul…

FIN

# EPILOGUE

I once read a newspaper article about a condition known as 'survivor guilt', which concerns those whose instinct in a calamity is so strong that they'll do anything to survive. This might mean crawling over the heads of other passengers in a smoke-filled aeroplane to reach the exits, or being the first man in the life-raft when it is supposed to be 'women and children only'. Who can know how you will react until such a time comes?

In some ways I suffered a little from survivor guilt after this trip, because despite choosing unlikely vehicles for the journey, very little went wrong with them. Those few things that did go wrong I'd either prepared for (like packing a spare oil pump), or were dealt with almost effortlessly (Maicitbetta's broken exhaust and blown fork gaskets). Beyond checking his wheel nuts in Austria, the only time Dean touched his scooter was to ride it or wash it.

From an 'overcoming adversity' point of view it doesn't make for the most adventurous read, but from a 'touring with kids' standpoint it was perfect. Certainly I wouldn't have wanted any extra breakdowns or incidents just to beef up our story.

What this lack of trauma proved was that the arduous months of planning, scooter preparation and saving up were all worthwhile. We'd kept all our promises to the kids, met every objective and emerged at the other end unscathed. That doesn't happen very often in life, so I guess there's no reason to feel guilty about it.

Even on a personal level we'd managed well, despite the unusual make-up of our travelling party and choice of transport. Having two headstrong characters in the same small group requires considerable diplomatic skill and patience, and only once had I unsettled that equilibrium. For the rest of the time it worked as an advantage. Both Dean and I were capable of taking up the reins if the other faltered. Either of us could read a map, book a hotel, put up a tent, fix a scooter, or come up with a workable plan to get us out of a hole. Tracy too is capable of all those things, except maybe the scooter repair. Having that level of redundancy in a group is very useful.

Below the surface there was a little more going on. Dean and I were testing the water for a bigger, bolder and more adventurous ride that we'd discussed in the past. This trip acted as an experiment in riding, navigating and problem solving together. I like to think that we both passed the test, which gives us a green light for further adventures.

What I didn't expect was that Dean's mind was already racing ahead, and in little more than a month I'd be back in Albania and northern Greece as part of a bigger group riding even smaller scooters.

But that's another story…

*Places as beautiful as this are only a scooter ride away, so what's stopping you?*

# APPENDIX:
## BUILDING YOUR OWN TOUR

If this book inspires fellow scooterists to prod the kickstart on their own travel adventures, then it will have hit its target. That's not an entirely magnanimous aim on my part because, rather selfishly, I still love hearing the inspirational tales of others. Their stories, in turn, will motivate me to get off my arse and get back on the road.

Should you decide to go touring the hard way, on a classic scooter rather than by BMW bike or Toyota Land Cruiser, then you'll need all the help you can get. Here are a few tips gleaned from years of scooter rallying and touring that might just come in handy:

## PLANNING

If you are the adventurous type then just grab your passport, point the front wheel towards the border and ride. For the rest of us, just a little planning in advance can make life a lot easier:

- Set an achievable target for the trip both in terms of available time and money. Then bank on it taking at the very least an extra couple of days and costing 30% more.
- Weigh-up your accommodation choices in terms of hotels, hostels or camping. A tent might be the cheapest and most flexible option, but it is heavy and constantly camping and de-camping can become monotonous.
- Make a plan for dealing with money: saving it up, carrying it, accessing it, swapping currencies and how to deal with lost bank cards etc.
- Research interesting places on your route in advance. It is surprisingly easy to ride straight past somewhere wonderful if you didn't know it existed.
- If you are a technophile, like me, then consider the issues of data storage and power for any rechargeable technology you plan to take, but always ensure you have a back-up plan. A smartphone with no charge is about as much use as pubes around your arsehole. Carrying paper maps and a written list of essential phone numbers is probably a wise precaution.

- Make sure that you are properly insured for your whole trip; not only in terms of vehicle insurance, but also travel insurance that covers scooter riding in all the countries you plan to visit. Boring as it sounds, that might mean reading the small print, because that's where insurance companies hide all those nasty exclusions.
- Take at least one set of photocopied documents as well as the originals. Carry each set separately but somewhere waterproof and easily accessible.
- Prepare for potential mechanical disasters before they happen. Box-up any heavy spares that you might need and arrange for a friend to post them to you if required.
- Think about protective clothing and riding gear. Don't forget anything essential, but equally don't bring something you'll never use. Take into account the widest range of weather conditions you might experience. Even in the height of summer it will be cold crossing mountains.
- Consider your breakdown recovery options in advance. Some insurance policies include European breakdown cover, but it can't hurt to take a list of scooter shops and clubs along your route to call on in times of need.
- Pick an achievable distance for each day with a target destination. If you are being extra-thorough, research alternative stop-overs both nearer and beyond your planned destination.
- Plan a short stint for the first day, because this is when most preparation problems will rear their heads.

## RIDING COMPANIONS

Nothing will affect your enjoyment of a road trip more than the people you decide to ride with, so chose well and try not to break them. You are all in it together, so a dose of awareness and compassion can go a long way.

- The smaller your riding group the more easily you will interact with people that you meet along the way. Big groups tend to be more insular and intimidating to outsiders, and are more likely to splinter if individuals cannot agree common targets.

- It's better to know your companions well before you leave. Know what makes them tick, what their objectives are, how they will react in stress situations and what makes them flip out.
- What are your companion's weaknesses? Do they have problems riding at night or in particular conditions? Do they lose patience when hungry or tired? How do they cope with the heat or the cold?
- As you need to make allowances for their weaknesses, equally you need to be open about your own so that they can do the same.
- Are there any physical or mental conditions that you should prepare for? Does anyone need regular medication and do you know how to treat them if they become ill?

# LUGGAGE

You will need a loading system for your scooter: preferably one that is safe, secure and also quickly applied. The novelty of loading and unloading complex arrangements of bags rapidly wears thin.

- Arrange all the stuff you think you'll need for the trip in a pile by the scooter: then put half of it back in the house. For example don't bring 14 pairs of socks, just bring a few pairs and buy some more on the way. There are no countries I know of where socks are expensive or hard to come by.
- Try to keep as much of the luggage weight between your wheel axles as possible. Anything you carry beyond those extremities will adversely affect the handling of the scooter.
- If you are carrying a lot of weight, don't forget to increase your tyre pressures to suit.
- Bring a small First Aid Kit for emergencies: compact versions are available specifically for motorcyclists.
- If you need to carry 2-stroke oil, put it in a plastic fuel can rather than carrying bottles that are prone to split. Oily underwear is sexy in very few situations.

- When it comes to attaching everything, webbing cargo straps are far more secure than bungees, but slow to use and need any loose ends securing. Bungees are quicker to use but leave luggage wobbly when loosely fastened. Tightly-pulled bungees can be really dangerous and prone to whipping people in the face. Elastic cargo nets are safer and often a good compromise.
- Never underestimate the usefulness of a Frisbee. It can be a plate, a parts tray, a dog bowl and even a throwable toy. Wash between uses though.

## SPARES TO BRING WHEN CLASSIC SCOOTER TOURING

- Set of spare bulbs.
- A clutch and brake lever: in case you drop your scooter.
- Cables: clutch, gear and throttle inners.
- M7 exhaust studs and nuts: this oddball thread size is fairly unique to Lambretta, Vespa and some Citroens.
- Specific Lambretta spares that Dean recommends to bring: an oil drain plug, a fuel tap and preferably a rear hub kept inside your spare wheel. All these parts are unique and difficult to manage without.
- In a small container bring spare woodruff keys for the engine, nipples for the cables, a selection of nuts and bolts and a few electrical crimp connectors.
- A spare set of oiled clutch plates in a plastic bag do not take up much space.
- If possible bring a spare wheel and an inner tube or puncture repair kit (tubeless wheels). On long tours expect to wear out and replace at least one tyre.

## GROUP SPARES AND TOOLS

- Bring special tools (flywheel extractor, clutch compressor etc), even if you don't know how to use them. They will be essential for anyone who works on your scooter.
- Divide the special tools between the bikes, because there's no point in duplicating what you carry.

- If going to somewhere remote, try to ensure that the scooters have exactly the same engine spec. For instance one spare piston or one hub will thus be of use to any of your party.
- Bring a tow rope: it is not always the safest or most legal method to deal with a breakdown, but it is often the quickest way to get off a dodgy bit of road to somewhere safer.
- General toolbox touring essentials are silicone instant gasket, cable ties, hose clips, insulation tape and gaffer tape. With this sort of stuff you can bodge the universe back together.

# ON THE ROAD

Setting off with a completely detailed schedule can quickly drain the fun out of things. Instead it's often better to improvise as you go along.

- Use free Wi-Fi access in hotels, petrol stations or fast food restaurants to book accommodation en route.
- If using a booking website, specify 'safe parking for X number of motorcycles' in the additional requirements section. If you get no confirmation, then this could be a handy get-out clause for rejecting unsatisfactory accommodation.
- For the same reason, don't book too many nights in one go. It's normally easy to add extra nights if you find somewhere you like and want to stay for longer.
- Think about security for the bikes and your belongings. Most places you'll visit will probably be fine (except for port towns), but still there is no room for complacency. Lock it or lose it.
- Choose your information sources carefully: try to spot outdated or prejudiced advice, and instead believe those who have recent personal experience.

# DEALING WITH PROBLEMS

A wise man once said: shit happens! You can't stop it but you can be ready for it. Try to agree solutions to potential problems beforehand and keep a close eye for tell-tale symptoms.

- Make sure each rider has a phone number for everyone else in the group and all the mobiles are set up for international calling.
- Ensure that everyone knows the name of the destination for that day in case you get split up. Ideally everyone should have a map or an app as well.
- When riding in a pack put someone who can navigate at the front, along with the slowest rider, and someone with mechanical skills at the back.
- If you break down and can't fix the bike immediately then send an SMS to the lead rider explaining where you are and what has happened. They should call back once they stop and realise that someone is missing.
- Watch out for a sudden slip in riding standard. Some people become erratic when they need food; others become drowsy at certain times in the afternoon or night. It's better to stop for a short break before it gets too dangerous.

# ESSENTIALS

- Take lots of photos and video as you go. Your memory will fade quicker than digital images ever will.
- **Along the way, take time to smell the flowers.**

# DEDICATION

For Sam and Kimberly: last of the petrol generation.